On Your Bike
in
The Cotswolds

On Your Bike
in
The Cotswolds

Ellen Lee and John Broughton

COUNTRYSIDE BOOKS
NEWBURY BERKSHIRE

COUNTRYSIDE BOOKS
3 Catherine Road
Newbury, Berkshire

To view our complete range of books,
please visit us at
www.countrysidebooks.co.uk

ISBN 1 85306 666 4

Designed by Graham Whiteman
Maps by Gelder design & mapping
Photographs by the authors

Produced through MRM Associates Ltd., Reading
Printed in Italy

CONTENTS

AREA MAP SHOWING THE LOCATIONS OF THE RIDES

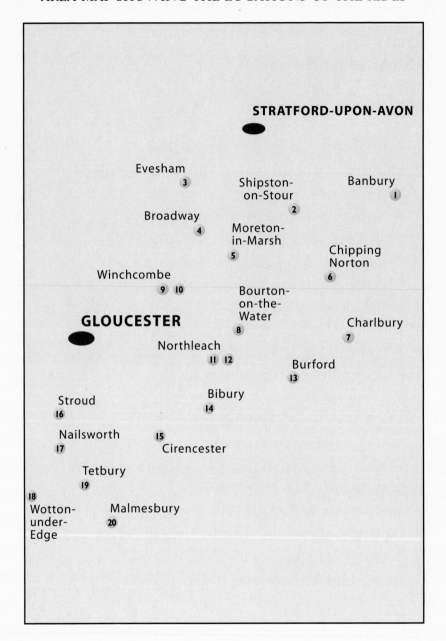

INTRODUCTION

C ycling is much more than a way of getting from A to B. Journeying by car, bus or train you exist in a state of limbo, places rushing past too fast to experience them and only start and destination having any solid reality. By bicycle, travelling becomes a complete sensory experience. You see, hear, smell and sometimes even touch your environment. You travel slowly enough to interact with your surroundings, to wave a greeting, to exchange a smile and to see those small details which help define each place as unique. Yet you travel quickly enough to see the subtle changes which mark out one area as distinct from the next.

These Cotswold rides span the counties of Gloucestershire, Worcestershire, Warwickshire, Oxfordshire and Wiltshire. You will find very many obvious similarities throughout the region, for example the many fine stone cottages, the small fast flowing streams and the open pastoral landscape. The area is steeped in history and the rides investigate the Cotswolds from the Neolithic and Bronze Ages, to medieval times, the turbulent years of the English Civil War and onwards to the Industrial Revolution and finally into the present.

The routes vary in distance from 13 to 26 miles and even with visits to places of interest and stops for refreshment, none should take more than five hours to complete. Being a hilly region, some of the rides are strenuous, and we have indicated the degree of difficulty in the preface to each ride. Be sensible about your choice of ride, but don't be put off, you can always push up a hill and ups are more often than not followed by downs! More than anything take the opportunity offered by cycling to explore the wonderful countryside, villages and towns you pass through.

Cycling is what you want it to be. Whether you like to ride on your own or with friends or family and whether you enjoy riding fast, savouring the physical pleasures of riding or prefer to potter around in a more leisurely fashion, stopping en route to investigate nooks and crannies and savour the sights, sounds and tastes of the country . . . whatever and however you do it, we hope that this book and its suggested routes inspire you with a taste for bicycle adventures.

Ellen Lee and John Broughton

GUIDE TO USING THIS BOOK

Each route is preceded by information to help you:

The **number of miles** is the total for the ride. Apart from short distances on tracks and a couple of routes with towpath sections, all the rides are on roads with hard surfaces.

The brief **introduction** to the ride gives a broad picture of where the route takes you and also mentions particular features you will see.

The **maps** listed at the beginning of each ride are all Ordnance Survey maps and it is advisable to take them with you as the sketch maps give limited information.

The **starting point** includes a suggested car park where you can leave your vehicle whilst on the ride.

Places for refreshment, sometimes particular pubs or tearooms, are mentioned in the pre-ride information and others are just waiting for you to discover them. Don't forget Paragraph 211 of the Highway Code: You MUST NOT ride under the influence of drink or drugs.

THE ROUTES

It is a good idea to read right through a route before setting out so that you note any places where you want to spend more time.

The directions have been written as clearly as possible. Instructions to turn left or right are printed in bold, like this:

Turn **L** at the T-junction; **bear R** when the road forks by the church. Instructions to continue straight over a crossroads or carry straight on are not in bold.

The directions include some description about the route, but at the end of each route there is more information about **places of interest**. These include notes about architecture, history, legends and people connected with each entry.

The map of the area on page 4 shows where the twenty routes are situated. Each route is accompanied by a simple **sketch map**. These maps are intended to give you a general idea of where the routes go but are not detailed enough to be route guides. The relevant OS Landranger Series map is always recommended.

BEFORE YOU START

This section is aimed at cyclists who have not ventured out on a touring ride before. It is important to go prepared so that if a problem occurs you are in a good position to cope with it. We have put together a few pointers to help you.

Firstly, make sure that your bicycle is in roadworthy condition. Check the tyres for wear, or damage, and make sure that they are properly inflated. Check the brakes. Change badly worn blocks. Cycling in hilly areas, such as the Cotswolds, the health of tyres and brakes is vitally important for your safety. Remember too that rain often washes sharp flints into the road which are particularly troublesome if your tyres are badly worn. Treat your bicycle as a friend and it will reward you with many miles of happy cycling.

Having made sure that your bicycle is well looked after, it is time to attend to your needs. Make sure that your bicycle is adjusted to suit you, as a wrongly adjusted machine can be very tiring and uncomfortable. A useful tip is to make sure when the saddle height is checked that the shoes you are wearing are the ones to be worn on the ride. The shoe sole thickness is important.

Always cycle in comfortable clothing, and go prepared with some waterproof clothing even if you think you won't need it. Do not ride with baggy trousers or long shoelaces as they can get caught between the chain and chain ring. If cycling in the winter take an extra layer of warm clothing as well, just in case the temperature drops unexpectedly. It is a good idea to carry a drink (water will do) and a snack to fend off thirst and hunger. Water bottle carriers can be fitted to any bicycle.

Other things to carry with you should include a basic toolkit, puncture outfit, tyre levers and a spare inner tube, not forgetting a suitable pump. Most experienced cyclists change the inner tube if they have a puncture as it is easier than mending the puncture on the road. Another reason for carrying a spare tube is that a puncture can occur in a place where it is not possible to stick on a patch.

If your wheels are fastened in using nuts rather than quick release mechanisms, make sure that the wheel nuts are not too tight for the spanner carried. It is a good idea to undo then retighten the nuts with the spanner in your toolkit which will ensure that you can loosen them if it becomes necessary.

Tip: *Make sure that your toolkit contains a pair of long nosed pliers which are very useful for pulling out thorns etc when they have caused a puncture.*

It is advisable to carry some money and identification, in case of emergency. Having taken these precautions you should be able to enjoy your cycle touring rides to the full, and with peace of mind.

All of these pointers are based upon experience gained from many thousands of cycling miles.

SAFETY
In general when cycling on a public highway obey the highway code, and use common sense. The wearing of helmets is not compulsory in the UK and is left to the discretion of the rider. It is a good idea to wear something light in colour so that other road users can see you. Remember that it is the responsibility of the cyclist to make him or herself visible, especially in low light. On some days when it is dark and wet it is sometimes advisable to use lights to make sure that you are seen, especially under the cover of trees.

1

Banburyshire and Civil War Battles

24 miles

This ride explores the countryside at the extreme north-eastern limit of the Cotswolds. In the villages, you will see that grey Cotswold stone has given way to orange marlstone, much of which was quarried locally. Starting from Banbury, the route heads north along the Oxford Canal to Cropredy, before turning west and climbing the escarpment to Edgehill. You return through the ironstone villages of Hornton and Wroxton, with a short detour to visit Broughton Castle. The ride has a strong Civil War theme as you pass through two of the most famous battle sites of the 'Oxford campaign'.

Map: OS Landranger 151 Stratford-upon-Avon (GR 462405).

Starting point: The ride starts from the railway station in Banbury, situated close to junction 11 of the M40, 20 miles north of Oxford. Parking is available in two car parks straddling the canal in the new Castle Quay development (GR 458407).

Refreshments: There are plenty of places to eat in Banbury itself. Around the route the Bridge Stores at Cropredy is useful for provisions. In Cropredy the Brasenose Arms and the Red Lion serve food. There is also the Green Scene coffee shop and art gallery. The Castle Inn at Edgehill is highly recommended for food, beer and the view. There is a tearoom at Broughton Castle (when open).

The route: The initial 6 miles uses canal towpath and passes through the gentle arable countryside of the Cherwell Valley. The towpath surface is generally good, although it can be narrow due to erosion. Please be considerate to pedestrians and fishermen. This is a ride of contrasts with some steepish climbs.

Starting from the station, follow the exit road to a T-junction. Cross the road (use the pedestrian crossing if necessary) and go through the gap in the railings onto a cycle track. **Bear L** when the track branches and soon **turn R** onto the towpath near where it passes under a road bridge. If you are starting from the Castle Quay car parks, join the canal towpath and head north (out of town). You will soon pass under another road bridge. Look ahead to your right, and you will see a cycle track heading through Spiceball Park. Take this track and by keeping left ride roughly parallel to the canal. After about ½ mile rejoin the towpath. Keep on the towpath till

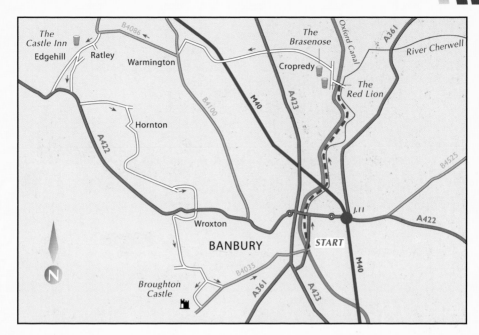

Cropredy Bridge (number 153), a distance of about 5 miles.

Leave the towpath at Cropredy Bridge. **Turn L** onto the road and cross the bridge. **Turn R** at the triangular junction (signed Mollington/Claydon). **Turn L** (signed Mollington) and climb the hill. The view back into the valley is well worth stopping to admire. At the staggered crossroads with the A423, **turn R** (signed Southam) and immediately **turn L** (signed Mollington). Ride through Mollington and continue to cross over the M40. Soon **turn R** at the T-junction (signed Warmington).

Ride into Warmington and **turn L** (signed Banbury/Warwick) to ride through the large village green with its stone cottages and raised

pond. The road soon starts to climb steeply (luckily there is a seat halfway up!) to meet the B4100. **Turn L** (signed Shotteswell/ Banbury). Soon, after the road has returned to single carriage, carefully **turn R** (signed Edgehill/ Kineton B4086). The effort of the climb is now rewarded with stunning views on both sides.

Turn L at the T-junction (signed Edgehill/Ratley). Soon you will enter Edgehill, with the Castle Inn to your right. The battlefield itself is down the escarpment between Radway and Kineton, and you can get wonderful views from the inn. **Turn L** (signed Leisure Drive). **Bear R** (signed Banbury) and at the T-junction with the A422, **turn L** (signed Banbury) and after ¼ mile **turn L** (signed Hornton). **Turn R**

Even the ducks have thatched cottages in Wroxton!

(signed Hornton) and ride down into and up out of the village. Continue and **turn L** (signed Horley/Hanwell). At the T-junction **turn R** (signed Wroxton) and **turn L** (not signed; if you meet the A422 here you have gone too far).

At the junction with the A422 **turn R** (not signed) and soon **turn L** (signed Wroxton only). Ride into the delightful village of Wroxton. Pass the church and continue up Main Street to the T-junction with the A422. **Turn L** (not signed) and soon **turn L** again (signed North Newington). Note the unusual stone guidepost at this junction. At the T-junction in Newington **turn L** (signed Newington/Banbury). If

you don't want to visit Broughton Castle, keep on this road and **turn L** at the T-junction with the B4035 (signed Banbury). Otherwise, outside the village **turn R** (signed Broughton) and soon **turn R** again (not signed). **Bear L** (signed the Oxfordshire Cycleway). The entrance to Broughton Castle is on your right. On leaving, continue on this road and **turn L** at the T-junction (signed B4035, Banbury).

Follow the B4035 into Banbury. Go straight on at the roundabout and proceed into the centre. At Banbury Cross (roundabout) go straight on and over one set of traffic lights. Whether you are heading for the station or Castle Quay **turn L** at the T-junction with traffic lights and get in the right-hand lane and **turn R** at the next set (signed the station). If you prefer, cross and push your bike over the road. If you are heading for the station, **turn R** into the station concourse, otherwise take the cycle track into the park as described at the start of the route and return to the canal towpath and car parks.

• •

THE CIVIL WAR BATTLES
The Battle of Edgehill in October 1642 was the first true (but unplanned) battle of the war. The two armies accidentally discovered that they were only 7 miles apart near Edgehill. The Parliamentarians were well armed but had poor morale and inexperienced commanders. The Royalist infantry had little more than pitchforks with which to fight, but were better motivated. The Royalists made the first move, coming down from the escarpment to fight on the low ground between Kineton and Radway. Modern estimates are that 1,500 men perished in the ensuing battle which was inconclusive although the Royalists received a morale boost when the Parliamentarians withdrew leaving them the spoils of the battlefield.

In June 1644, the Parliamentary army commanded by Waller arrived at Hanwell Castle while harrying the King's Oxford army. The Royalists marched to meet them but decided not to engage, and continued northwards. However, mindful that there were several crossing places of the river Cherwell, and not wishing to be attacked in their flanks, the King ordered his army to march rapidly to the bridge

The Castle Inn, Edgehill

at Cropredy. Unfortunately, his rearguard did not receive the order and a mile long gap opened up. This tempted Waller to cross the Cherwell at Slat Bridge (south of Cropredy) and attack. However, the Royalists were too strong and too determined and inflicted a defeat precipitating the collapse of Waller's army.

BROUGHTON CASTLE

Broughton Castle, the home of Lord Saye and Sele (the Fiennes family) for 600 years, is a moated manor house located near the village of Broughton, 3 miles south-west of Banbury. It is most famously associated with the Civil War. Before the opening of hostilities, meetings of the Providence Island Trading Company were a front for secret talks among the King's opponents. The Castle may be visited from mid May to mid September, Wednesdays and Sundays (also Thursdays in July and August) and Bank Holiday Sundays and Mondays (including Easter) 2 pm to 5 pm. An entrance fee is charged.

2

Shipston-on-Stour: Vales, Hills and Gardens

23 miles

This ride starts in Shipston-on-Stour and heads north along the gently undulating Stour valley to the beautiful village of Halford. It then turns westwards towards the most northerly outcrop of the Cotswold hills, passing through Ilmington with its two large village greens, golden stone houses and orchards. The route then climbs towards Hidcote Bartrim where the two 'Arts and Crafts' gardens at Kiftsgate Court and Hidcote Manor can be visited. It continues through Ebrington and to the eastern edge of the hills overlooking the Stour valley. A descent back to river level soon returns us to Shipston-on-Stour.

Map: OS Landranger 151 Stratford-upon-Avon (GR 259405).

Starting point: The ride starts from the main square in the centre of Shipston-on-Stour, outside the White Bear Hotel. There is plenty of free parking. We recommend using the Telegraph Street car park off the main A3400, just north of the town centre. The main square can be accessed on foot from this car park via a passageway adjacent to the Museum. The nearest railway station to the route is Honeybourne on the line between London Paddington and Worcester.

Refreshments: Shipston-on-Stour has several pubs, hotels and a teashop (weekdays only) in the main square. The Red Lion at Ilmington serves bar meals, and about halfway around there are both tearooms and a licensed restaurant at Hidcote Gardens (National Trust).

The route: The ride is quite hilly, although none of the hills are very long, and the views are well worth the effort, especially on a clear day when you may even be able to spot the Malvern Hills.

From the White Bear Hotel in the main square **turn L** (with your back to the hotel) onto New Street. Go straight across at the give way line and get in the right-hand lane and **turn R** opposite the Horseshoe (signed Banbury/Oxford). Soon **turn L** (signed Brailes/Banbury B4035). Cross the River Stour on

the stone bridge and soon **turn L** (signed Honington). At the following T-junction **turn L** (signed Honington). In Honington itself **turn R** at the T-junction (signed Idlicote/Whatcote) and soon **turn L** (signed Halford).

Shortly after passing Parkhill Farm

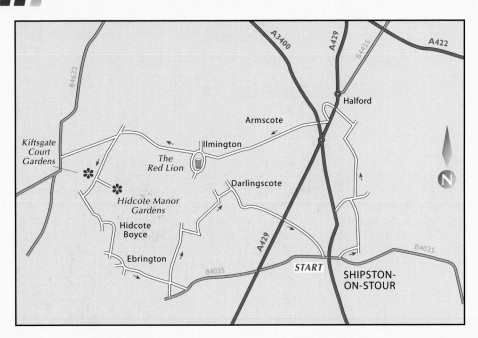

turn **L** (signed Halford) and proceed to the junction with the A429. Cross straight over (with care) into Queen Street and ride through the lovely unspoilt village. Queen Street runs parallel to the A-road and eventually rejoins it. Either **turn R** onto the A429 and just the other side of the Halford Bridge Inn **turn R** (not signed, no through road) or if you prefer push your bicycle along the pavement, past the inn and ride down the no through road.

Soon you will cross the original packhorse bridge, much mended after the trials and tribulations of the Civil War. If the farm gate is shut, push your bicycle through the barrier. **Turn R** at the T-junction (not signed). Go carefully straight on at the

crossroads with the A3400 (signed Armscote/Ilmington). Ride straight through Armscote keeping on the same road and ride into Ilmington.

At the T-junction **turn L** (signed Chipping Campden). Ride past Lower Green and up past the Red Lion pub and on and upwards. Soon you will reach Upper Green. **Turn R** (Back Street). You will see the church and an orchard on your right. At the T-junction **turn L** (signed Admington/Mickleton). Keep on this road for about 1½ miles. On a sharp left-hand bend you will see a turn to the right to Stratford. *Don't* take this turn, but shortly **turn L** (signed Hidcote Gardens/Kiftsgate Gardens). Climb the hill. The first part is steep, but it soon flattens out to give wonderful views back towards

Hidcote Manor and Gardens

Edgehill and forward and right towards Bredon Hill and the Vale of Evesham.

The entrance to Kiftsgate Gardens is on the right, and shortly the turn for Hidcote Gardens is to your left. If you want to visit Hidcote Gardens **turn L** here otherwise keep straight on (signed Hidcote Boyce). **Turn L** (signed Hidcote Boyce/Ilmington) and ride through the village and climb out to a T-junction. Here **turn R** (signed Ebrington/Chipping Campden). **Turn L** at the crossroads (signed Ebrington/Shipston-on-Stour). Go straight on at the give way sign in Ebrington (signed Charingworth) and ride through the village following signs for Charingworth. Ride into Charingworth. **Turn L** (not signed) up a narrow wooded hill soon passing Magpie Cottage on your right. At the top of the rise you will see the two masts at the top of Nebworth Hill ahead of you and a little further on you will pass a pick-your-own soft fruit farm (open during the summer, and offering quite a variety of different temptations!).

Turn R (not signed) and descend the hill with care. After about a mile, **turn R** (signed Darlingscote) and at the T-junction **turn R** (signed Darlingscote, marked as National Cycle Network route 5). **Bear L** (signed Shipston) and ride through Darlingscote. Cross straight over the A429 at the crossroads (signed Shipston). Ride

into Shipston-on-Stour. **Turn L** at the T-junction (signed Banbury, B4035, West Street). If you wish to return to the main square it will soon appear to your left. Otherwise, to return to the car park, go straight on at the give way line and **turn L** (opposite the Horseshoe) and **turn L** (Telegraph Street). The car park is soon on your left.

● ●

TWO COTSWOLD GARDENS

This ride is fortunate in passing two magnificent Cotswold gardens which are regularly open to the public. Their designs were both strongly influenced by the Arts and Craft movement which was so much part of the Cotswolds at the end of the 19th century. **Kiftsgate Court Gardens** are the work of three generations of women gardeners beginning with Heather Muir who bought the house in 1918. The plan is of a series of interconnecting gardens each designed with colour and pattern in mind, and many reflecting her passion for roses. The nearby **Hidcote Manor Gardens** (NT) are the work of Major Lawrence Johnston. His use of space, hedges, walls, paving and water in what might be termed 'total garden design' was very innovative at the time (over 70 years ago). Kiftsgate Court is open in April, May, August and September on Wednesdays, Thursdays and Sundays and Bank Holiday Mondays 2 pm to 6 pm and in June and July on Wednesdays, Thursdays, Saturdays and Sundays 12 noon to 6 pm. For opening times of Hidcote Manor Gardens, please ring 01684 855370. Both gardens charge an entrance fee.

3

The Vale of Evesham

20 miles

Although strictly speaking not in the Cotswolds, the escarpment provides an ever present backdrop to this gentle ride. It starts in the delightful town of Evesham which sits astride the River Avon, and whose town centre is graced by many distinguished old buildings, some of which were once part of the Abbey. The route meanders around the Vale, through orchards and fields growing a great variety of crops from parsley to pumpkins. The pretty villages are an interesting mixture of Cotswold stone, red brick, half-timber and thatch. At Middle Littleton you can visit the magnificent tithe barn, a cathedral of a building and at Honeybourne you can visit the Domestic Fowl Trust and its collection of rare breeds of chickens, ducks, geese and turkeys.

Map: OS Landranger 150 Worcester and The Malverns (GR 040437).

Starting point: This ride starts from Workman Bridge, which is the main bridge over the River Avon in the centre of Evesham. There are two well-signed car parks, one to the west of the A4184 (Merstow Green), High Street, and the other on the left immediately after crossing Workman Bridge from the B4035. Evesham can be reached by railway from Worcester and from London Paddington and Oxford. From the railway station head south on the A4184. Workman Bridge is at the bottom of Bridge Street, a turning to the east off High Street (A4184).

Refreshments: Evesham has plenty of pubs, cafés, and tearooms. Around the route, food is served at the Ivy Inn (North Littleton), the King's Arms (Cleeve Prior) and the Thatched Tavern (Honeybourne). Drinks and cakes are also available at the Domestic Fowl Trust in Honeybourne.

The route: The ride is flat except for a couple of gentle climbs and is mostly on quiet country lanes. However, care should be exercised on the 3 mile section of the B4035 between Bretforton and Evesham which can sometimes be busy. Unfortunately at present there is no quieter route into Evesham.

From Workman Bridge, head in an easterly direction (out of town). Go straight over at the traffic lights to enter the Begeworth area of Evesham. **Turn L** at the roundabout (signed Badsey/ Offenham). **Turn L** down Offenham Road (signed Offenham). Cross the A46 on a bridge and you will soon find yourself amid orchards and fruit farms where in autumn you can weigh yourself down by picking your own apples and pears. Cross

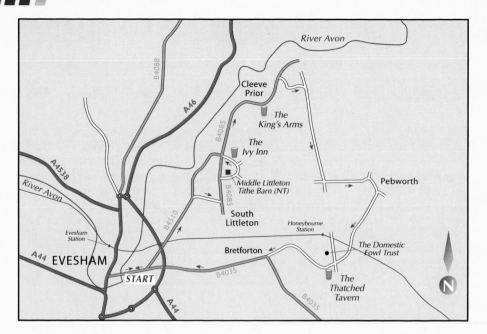

the railway line and enter Offenham. Keep on through the village on the B4510. Outside the village **turn R** into Bennets Hill (signed The Littletons). Climb the hill and enter South Littleton. You should get a good view of the Cotswold escarpment to your right.

At the T-junction **turn L** onto the B4085 (signed North Littleton/ Cleeve Prior). On entering Middle Littleton take the first **turn R** onto School Lane (signed Tithe Barn). Soon after a sharp left-hand bend look out for a small road leading to your left (signed The Barn). Follow this road around to the right through some farm buildings to visit the magnificent medieval Tithe Barn.

When you are ready, rejoin the road and continue towards North Littleton. **Turn L** at a triangular green (signed Offenham/Evesham). Soon **turn L** again passing the Ivy Inn. At the crossroads **turn R** back onto the B4085 (signed Cleeve Prior). Ride into and through Cleeve Prior and into the edge of Marlcliff. **Turn R** (signed Bickmarsh). As you climb the hill look back and you will see the town of Bidford-on-Avon behind you. At the following T-junction **turn R** (not signed).

Ride past the Bidford Gliding Club and into Ullington. **Turn L** at the crossroads (signed Pebworth/Broad Marston/Mickleton). Ride into Pebworth and **turn R** by the church onto Front Street (signed Broad Marston). Follow the road to the edge of the village and **turn R**

The half-timbered buildings of Evesham

(signed Honeybourne). If you wish to visit the Domestic Fowl Trust **turn R** at the crossroads in Honeybourne (200 yards on your left) otherwise go straight on (signed Village Centre/Evesham). Ride into Bretforton and **turn R** onto the B4035 (signed Evesham). Keep on this road through Badsey, and with care go straight over at the roundabout with the A46 (signed Evesham). **Turn R** at the following roundabout (signed Town Centre) and go straight on at the traffic lights to return to Workman Bridge.

EVESHAM

Evesham is a gem of a town, surrounded on three sides by the River Avon, and still dominated by the ruins of its once powerful Abbey. The bell tower, built in the Perpendicular style, still stands on the terrace overlooking the river on which the rest of the Abbey, founded in AD 714 by Egwin, Bishop of Worcester once stood. Nowadays there is a delightful series of gardens where the monks once worked and worshipped leading down to the river with its resident population of ducks and geese, a pleasant spot for a picnic. Almost every street in the town centre contains wonderful old buildings, many of them black and white timber-framed. The 14th-century Almonry on Vine Street now houses the local history museum.

The Bell Tower, the only surviving part of Evesham Abbey

MIDDLE LITTLETON TITHE BARN

Standing in the middle of this magnificent 136 foot long, 13th-century tithe barn with its 40 foot high oak pillars gives you a really good appreciation of the power that the medieval church wielded in this country. They laid claim to 10% of all the produce of the area, and clearly they needed a lot of room to store it all. The huge oak doors allowed ready passage of fully laden carts in and empty ones out, and the crook-beamed high oak roof created optimum space. Today we see it as our distant ancestors probably never did, empty, which strongly enhances its ecclesiastical origins.

THE DOMESTIC FOWL TRUST

If you think you know what a chicken looks like, you may be in for a surprise, because here at the Domestic Fowl Trust they come in many shapes and sizes. The Trust keeps a large number of domestic breeds of chickens, ducks, turkeys and geese and also some sheep, pigs and goats. Wandering around the many spacious pens is a good lesson in man's ability to manipulate nature without any need for genetic engineering! There is a picnic area, and there are usually plenty of chicks to watch and delight the children. The Trust is open from 10.30 am to 5 pm daily and an entrance fee is charged.

4
Broadway and Golden Stone Villages

13 miles

This ride starts in Broadway, a large show village at the base of the Cotswold escarpment. The route heads south-west, offering fine views of the wrinkled escarpment edge. Soon it starts climbing gently through the beautiful villages of Stanton and Stanway where the Jacobean mansion and gardens may sometimes be visited. For steam train enthusiasts, a ride on the scenic Gloucestershire and Warwickshire Railway is only a short detour away. The route continues to the picturesque village of Snowshill and a chance to visit the eccentric collection of Charles Padget Wade housed in Snowshill Manor, before an exhilarating descent down the old turnpike road back to Broadway.

Maps: OS Landranger 150 Worcester and The Malverns or OS Touring Map 8 The Cotswolds (GR 093376).

Starting point: This ride starts from the War Memorial on the village green at the western end of Broadway High Street, some 16 miles north-east of Cheltenham, just off the A44. There is long-stay car parking on the Childswickham Road (just off the B4632 Cheltenham road). Alternatively if you are visiting Snowshill Manor, you can park in the National Trust car park and start the ride from there. The nearest train station is Honeybourne, on the line between London Paddington and Worcester (Thames Trains) some 5 miles away. Alternatively, bicycles may be hired from Broadway Cycle Hire in Aston Somerville, about 2 miles off the B4632, west of Broadway (telephone: 01386 852754).

Refreshments: Broadway contains many pubs, restaurants, hotels and tearooms. The large village green has plenty of benches and is a fine place for a picnic. Snowshill Manor has a restaurant which serves light lunches and teas, and pub lunches are available at the Snowshill Arms in the village. The Manor's car park with its grassy banks and views of the escarpment is another good picnic site.

The route: There is one significant climb out of about 500 feet up the escarpment. This is almost entirely on the B4077 which is by far the most easily graded road up. You may find a steady stream of traffic going past. Nevertheless, it is a pleasantly wooded road with frequent pull-ins and regular views to reward your efforts. Once at the top, the route is very gently undulating and you have the pleasure of anticipating an exhilarating descent back to Broadway.

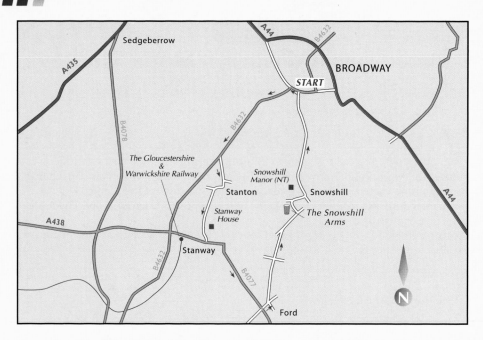

From the War Memorial, join the B4632 (High Street) and proceed in a westerly direction away from the centre of the village. **Turn L** (signed Winchcombe, B4632). Keep on this road for about 2¼ miles and then **turn L** (signed Stanton). Ride into this delightful village whose main street heads up the hill and is well worth exploring. **Bear R** (signed Stanway). Once clear of the village **turn L** (signed Stanway/ Stow-on-the-Wold). Pass the entrance to Stanway House on your left, and continue to a wooded cross-roads. The war memorial on your left to 'The Men of Stanway' is in the form of a bronze sculpture of St George and the Dragon by Alexander Fisher on a plinth designed by Sir Philip Stott. If you wish to take a ride on the Gloucestershire & Warwickshire

Railway **turn R**. The Toddington station is just over ½ mile on your left.

Otherwise **turn L** (signed Stow, B4077). The road soon starts the steady mile-long climb. At the top, shortly after passing the sign for the village of Ford, **turn L** (signed Cutsdean/Taddington/Snowshill). **Turn L** at the crossroads (signed Taddington/Broadway). Ride through Taddington and keep on this road for about 1½ miles. Then **turn L** (signed Snowshill/ Broadway). You will soon enter the pretty village of Snowshill. Ride past the church and continue following signs for Broadway. The entrance to Snowshill Manor is just outside the village on your left.

When you are ready to continue,

Snowshill Manor

rejoin the road (by turning left out of the National Trust car park) or otherwise keep straight on, and descend carefully back into Broadway. You will pass the old Norman church of St Eadburgha on your left and soon after enter Broadway. Follow the road to return to the High Street.

SNOWSHILL MANOR

Charles Padget Wade was a compulsive collector. He began at the age of seven and continued till his death in 1956. Throughout this period his collecting was guided by ideas of design, craftsmanship and colour. In 1951 he gave Snowshill Manor to the National Trust and he personally arranged items in each of the rooms. The result is fascinating, with

surprises around every corner, and something to suit every taste and interest. The gardens are set out in the cottage garden style, in a series of outdoor rooms which exude tranquillity. The property is a very popular one with visitors, so if you are able, visit it on a weekday when it is quieter. It is open Wednesday to Sunday from 11 am to 5 pm from the beginning of April to the end of October. Entrance to the house is by timed ticket. An entrance fee is charged.

STANWAY HOUSE

Stanway House is built on land originally bestowed on Tewkesbury Abbey. The house, gatehouse, church and medieval tithe barn are clustered together in parkland at the base of the Cotswold escarpment. The present house was built by the Tracey family over the period 1580–1640 and is made from golden

Cotswold stone. Some Elizabethan features remain although the effect is predominantly Jacobean. The 18th-century gardens rise up towards the escarpment and contain a pyramid folly built by Robert Tracy in 1750 honouring his father John Tracy, and a recently restored cascade and 70 foot fountain. The house and gardens are open to the public on Tuesday and Thursday afternoons from June to September. An entrance fee is charged.

THE GLOUCESTERSHIRE & WARWICKSHIRE RAILWAY

The Gloucestershire & Warwickshire Railway was formed with the aim of one day restoring the former GWR mainline between Stratford Race Course and Cheltenham Race Course. At present the society owns the trackbed between Broadway and Cheltenham Race Course and has spent the past 14 years setting up its base at Toddington and restoring 6½ miles of track from Toddington to Gotherington, just north of Bishops Cleeve. The 1¼ hour return trip offers wonderful views of the Cotswold escarpment and takes you back to the golden age of steam. Details of current train times and fares may be obtained by phoning 01242 621405 or a full timetable is available from the GWR website (www.gwsr.plc.uk). It is not necessary to book tickets in advance except for special events.

Moreton-in-Marsh: The Classic Cotswolds

21 miles

The market town of Moreton-in-Marsh lies in the quiet Evenlode valley. The route starts by climbing to the estate village of Batsford before turning along a ridge offering wide views north along the valley. It then descends before climbing to the delightful village of Blockley which will reward the time taken to explore it. It then continues to climb until you find yourself looking down on Broad Campden in the foreground and Chipping Campden's magnificent church in the background. Chipping Campden with its market cross, craft shops and buildings of beautiful honey-coloured Cotswold stone retains its charm and is a natural place for a break. The route returns through Todenham and Great Wolford and along quiet wooded roads into Moreton-in-Marsh.

Maps: OS Landranger 151 Stratford-upon-Avon or OS Touring Map 8 The Cotswolds (GR 205325).

Starting point: The ride starts from the Bear Inn at Moreton-in-Marsh which stands on the A44, 17 miles north-east of Cheltenham and 14 miles south of Stratford-upon-Avon. The town is served by the train line from London Paddington to Worcester. There is plenty of free car parking, both along the main street (A429, Fosse Way) and near the railway station. Alternatively it is possible to hire bicycles from the Country Lanes Cycle Centre adjacent to the railway station.

Refreshments: Moreton-in-Marsh and Chipping Campden offer a wide choice of eating places. Elsewhere there are a tearoom and several pubs in Blockley, the Baker's Arms in Broad Campden and the Fox and Hounds in Great Wolford.

The route: The ride is moderately hilly but there is never any shortage of scenery to admire.

If you arrive by train, exit the station and **bear L** and soon **bear R** with the Royal British Legion building to your right. **Turn R** (not signed) and then **turn L** at the T-junction with the A429. The Bear Inn is to your left.

Otherwise the ride starts from outside the Bear Inn on the main A429. With your back to the inn, cross the main road and proceed right (in a northerly direction) along the A429. Just before the railway bridge, **turn L** (signed

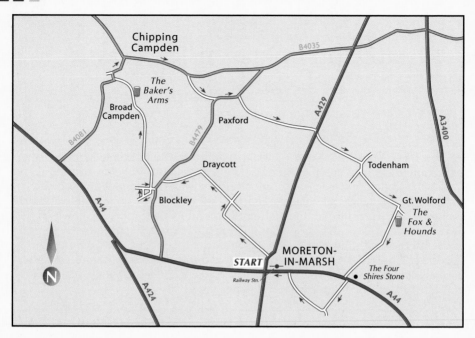

Batsford village only). In Batsford **bear R** (signed Aston Magna/ Chipping Campden). At the cross-roads **turn L** (signed Draycott/ Chipping Campden). In Draycott **bear L** (signed Blockley/Chipping Campden). Soon you will see the village of Blockley on the opposite hill.

In Blockley **turn L** at the T-junction (signed Bourton-on-the-Hill/Moreton). **Turn R** at the crest of the hill (signed Blockley Village). **Turn L** at the T-junction and follow the winding and narrow road through the village then **turn R** up Chapel Lane (signed Broadway). At the T-junction **turn R** (signed Northwich/Chipping Campden). **Turn L** at the next T-junction, Park Road (not signed).

This road climbs until at its top you get a wonderful, panoramic view. Descend the steep hill carefully into Broad Campden. **Turn L** at the T-junction (signed Broad Campden/Chipping Campden). Enjoy the well manicured hedges as you ride through the village! On the edge of Chipping Campden **turn R** at the T-junction (signed Shipston-on-Stour/Stratford-upon-Avon). At the T-junction in the centre **turn R** (signed Mickleton/Broadway). **Turn R** down Cidermill Lane (signed Ebrington/Paxford). **Turn L** down Station Road (signed Ebrington/ Paxford) and ride out of Chipping Campden.

Cross the railway line, and soon, **turn R** on a left-hand bend (signed

The Market Cross, Chipping Campden

Paxford). In Paxford **turn L** at the T-junction (signed Charingworth/Shipston-on-Stour, B4479). At the top of the ensuing climb **turn R** (signed Ditchford). At the T-junction with the A429 **turn R** (signed Stow), then soon **turn L** (signed Todenham/Great Wolford).

In Todenham **turn R** at the T-junction (signed Great Wolford). Soon **turn L** (signed Great Wolford). In Great Wolford **bear R** along the main road (signed Little Wolford/Barton). **Turn R** at the crossroads (signed Moreton). At the T-junction with the A44 **turn L** (signed Oxford). On this corner stands the Four Shires Stone, which marks the point where Oxfordshire, Worcestershire, Warwickshire, and

Gloucestershire used to meet. Almost immediately **turn R** (signed Evenlode). At the T-junction **turn R** (signed Moreton-in-Marsh). Ride into Moreton-in-Marsh then **turn L** at the T-junction with the A44 and ride back into the centre of town. If you wish to return to the railway station look out for signs to the station off to your right.

● ●

CHIPPING CAMPDEN

Take a while before you speed down the hill into Chipping Campden to admire it from afar. The huge Perpendicular-style parish church dominates the scene, and is probably the most magnificent of all the Cotswold 'Wool' churches. Once in the village, the site of the early 17th century Market Hall brings the realisation

The clipped yew hedges of Broad Campden

that all this is the product of centuries of trading, initially in wool and later in cheese and other dairy products. It is a popular tourist destination, and can be very busy in the summer and at weekends, so don't expect to have it to yourself. Despite this, half an hour or so on foot exploring the village is well worthwhile. Walking guides may be obtained from the Tourist Information Centre on High Street. At the turn of the 20th century many artisans arrived in Chipping Campden from London, inspired by the ideals of the Arts and Crafts movement. Many didn't survive the economic depression of the 1920s and the suspicion of the local people, but the legacy of the endeavour still lives on

in the Guild of Handicraft Trust which regularly mounts exhibitions in the Old Silk Mill in Sheep Street.

BLOCKLEY

This is one of my favourite Cotswold villages, hidden on the steep slopes of a hollow in one of the high wolds. The small stream flowing through the village provided the power to run six silk mills at the height of the village's prosperity in the early years of the 19th century when it supplied most of the raw material for the Coventry silk ribbon industry. Many of the most magnificent houses in the village date from this period, and it is always a pleasure to explore its narrow streets.

Chipping Norton and the Northern Cotswolds

20 miles

Starting from Chipping Norton, the highest town in Oxfordshire, the route explores the countryside to the north, in the transition zone between Cotswold stone and the orange marlstone, typical of the Banbury area. Lovers of real ale will want to take time to visit the Hook Norton Brewery and sample its products (although beware, it slips down deceptively well!). The route then swings north through a lovely group of villages, the Sibfords, before turning south to visit the prehistoric Rollright Stones.

Maps: OS Landranger 164 Oxford, Chipping Norton and Bicester and 151 Stratford-upon-Avon (GR 314273).

Starting point: This ride starts outside the Tourist Information Centre on Middle Row in Chipping Norton. Chipping Norton is located on the A44, 20 miles north-west of Oxford. The closest railway station is Kingham (London Paddington to Worcester Line), 5 miles to the south-west. There is ample and well-signed free parking. We recommend you use the long-term parking in Regent Court, just to the south of the A44.

Refreshments: Chipping Norton offers a good variety of eateries. We recommend the Old Mill Coffee Shop and Restaurant on West Street (B4450) and the Blue Boar Inn near the Tourist Information Centre. Along the route we recommend the Pear Tree in Hook Norton and the Bishop Blaize Inn at Burdrop. The Wyatts Countryside Centre just before the Rollright Stones is a good place to stop for a light meal or a drink.

The route: It must be admitted that what this route is not, is flat! In fact when you are not going up, you are invariably going down. Don't be put off though because you will be rewarded with good views of neighbouring valleys and the villages encountered are full of fine old buildings.

Turn R with your back to the Tourist Information Centre and soon **turn R** (Market Street). At the bottom of the hill, **turn R** (keeping the Chequers pub on your right) into Spring Street. **Turn L** at the T-junction (not signed). Keep on this road (the B4026) through the village of Over Norton and on to the T-junction with the A3400. **Turn L** (signed Long Compton) and immediately **turn R** (signed

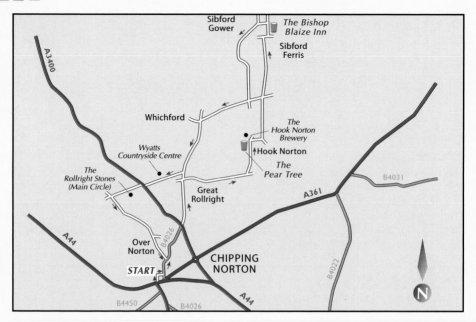

Great Rollright). Ride through Great Rollright and at the crossroads on the far edge of the village **turn R** (signed Hook Norton/Swerford).

After nearly 2 miles, **bear L** keeping on the same road (signed Hook Norton). Descend a steep hill into the village. At the bottom you will pass the Pear Tree pub on your left. If you wish to visit the Brewery, **turn L** by the pub, and soon **turn L** again (Brewery Lane). The Brewery is at the end of this lane. Otherwise **bear R** (signed Hook Norton). This road soon turns into High Street and you will pass the church on your left. Soon **turn L** (Queen Street). **Turn L** at the T-junction (not signed) and then **turn L** again (not signed, Sibford Road).

Continue on to the next crossroads with The Gate Hangs High pub ahead of you. Go straight over (signed Sibford Ferris/Swalcliffe). **Bear R** in Sibford Ferris (signed Banbury) and **turn L** (signed Burdrop). Descend a steep hill and climb out the other side. You will pass the Bishop Blaize Inn on your right. **Bear L** (signed Sibford Gower) and soon enter the village. **Turn L** at the crossroads (signed Hook Norton/Temple Mill). The road now descends into a lovely valley and climbs steadily out to a staggered crossroads next to The Firs Garage. **Turn R** (signed Whichford/Rollrights).

Climb a steep hill and at the top **bear L** (signed Great Rollright). Take time to admire the view to your right you have worked hard

Leaving Great Rollright

for. You will find yourself looking across the Evenlode valley towards Batsford and the hilly ridge you ride along in the early part of the ride from Moreton-in-Marsh, which is itself hidden in the valley. **Turn R** (signed Little Rollright/Stow) and soon pass Wyatts Countryside Centre on your right. The village you can see way down the hill to your right is Long Compton.

At the junction with the A3400, **turn R** (signed Long Compton/ Stratford) and immediately **turn L** (signed Little Rollright). The Rollright Stones are about ½ mile along this road on both sides (the main stone circle is to the left). On leaving the Rollright Stones

continue along the road till you reach a crossroads. **Turn L** (signed Little Rollright/Chipping Norton). Descend the steep hill carefully, and climb out the other side. Just before the top of the hill **turn R** (signed Over Norton). At the following T-junction, **turn R** (signed Chipping Norton). **Turn R** at the double mini-roundabout in Chipping Norton (signed A44, Evesham) to return to the start.

• •

CHIPPING NORTON

In Norman times, the manor of Norton, as it was then known, was located at the bottom of the hill, between the church and the brook. Here, in around 1120, a sizeable motte and bailey castle was built. Now all that remain are some earthworks,

33

and Pool Meadow, once a medieval fishpond. In 1205 it was decided to build a new market place, in its present position at the top of the hill, to help promote trade. King John granted a charter to hold a fair which made the town wealthy because they could charge tolls to trade. Soon the most wealthy citizens were building magnificent houses, paying to improve the church, building almshouses and a school. Today many of these buildings remain, although sometimes they have been altered according to the fashion. In the 19th century, Chipping Norton was a thriving town, its economy dominated by the Bliss Tweed Mill, brewing and glove making.

THE ROLLRIGHT STONES

The Rollright Stones consist of three main features, located within about 200 yards of each other on a ridge between Over Norton and Long Compton. Tradition has it that they represent a king, some of his treacherous knights and men who were turned to stone during a confrontation with a witch. However in reality, the stone circle, the King's Stone and the Whispering Knights date from different periods and their close proximity seems to be due to our ancestors' penchant for reusing old sacred sites. Indeed, there are also less obvious Roman and Saxon features close by, so the trend continued. The oldest of the three is the Whispering Knights, believed to be a 'Portal Dolmen' burial chamber, in use from 3800–3000 BC. The stone circle itself (the most easterly in the country) originally consisted of 105 stones (all local to the site) which formed a continuous ring with a single entrance. The circle is big enough to hold 200 people, although we have no knowledge of what (if any) ceremonies took place there. Finally, the King's Stone is believed to have marked a Bronze Age burial site.

Charlbury: Riding Through a Prehistoric Landscape

21 miles

This ride explores some of the open and less well-visited Cotswold countryside to the north-west of Charlbury. Be prepared for several long climbs and exhilarating descents on quiet roads. Take time off to investigate the peaceful stone villages and the many prehistoric remains. The halfway point at Churchill offers the opportunity to explore a prototype of Magdalen Tower in Oxford, and to picnic amid the stone monuments on the village green.

Maps: OS Landranger 163 Cheltenham and Cirencester and 164 Oxford, Chipping Norton and Bicester (GR 352194).

Starting point: This ride starts from Charlbury railway station. Charlbury is located 7 miles north of Witney and 15 miles north-east of Oxford. It may be reached by train from stations between London Paddington and Worcester. Cars may be parked in the Spendlove Car Park on the Enstone Road (B4022).

Refreshments: Food is available at several places throughout the route. We recommend the Coffee House and Restaurant (not Sundays) and the Bell Hotel, both in Charlbury and the Tite Inn in Chaddlington. Alternatively the village green in Churchill is a good place for a picnic.

The route: There are several climbs mostly in open country. Take the climbs gently, and you will be rewarded with several long freewheels downhill where you can feel the wind in your hair, and take in the scenery.

To get to the railway station from the car park, **turn R** (Browns Lane). At the staggered crossroads in the centre of Charlbury, **turn R** (signed Chipping Norton/Burford). **Turn L** and follow the signs for the railway station which is shortly on your left.

Ride out of the station, **turn L** at the T-junction with the B4437 (not signed) and start a steady climb. As you climb watch the scenery gradually unfold in typical rolling Cotswold fashion. After 2 miles, **turn R** (signed Chilson). Descend into the village and ride through continuing the descent. After you reach the valley bottom there is a long, steady climb out. At the top of this climb, and within sight of the T-junction with the A361,

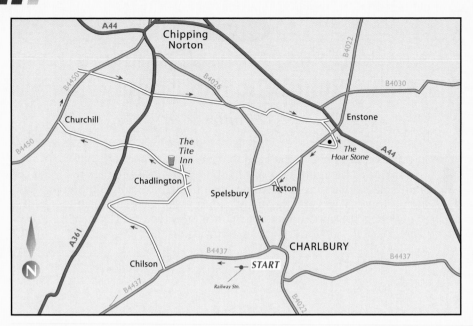

turn R (signed Chadlington). After the efforts of the climb you are rewarded by a long descent into Chadlington.

In Chadlington **turn L** by a garage (signed Chipping Norton/Churchill). **Turn L** (signed Churchill). A short distance along this road you will see the Tite Inn on the right. Near the top of the climb away from the village there is an earthworks on the right-hand side of the road. This ancient monument is known as Knowlbury and is a prehistoric burial ground.

At the T-junction **turn L** (signed Burford, A361) and **immediately turn R** (signed Churchill). **Bear R** (signed Sarsden/Churchill). Towards the end of the descent Churchill church suddenly comes into view.

The tower was designed as a prototype for the tower at Magdalen College in Oxford. **Turn R** onto the B4450 following signs for Chipping Norton. On your right is the village green with some interesting monuments, an ideal place for a picnic. When you are ready, continue on this road, riding out of the village.

Turn R at the crossroads (signed Lidstone). Chipping Norton can be seen on your left. The Bliss Tweed Mill (now converted into apartments) is the most prominent building. Go straight over at the crossroads with the A361 (signed Lidstone). At the T-junction **turn R** (not signed). Should you wish to return more directly to Charlbury, keep on this road through Spelsbury and back to Charlbury,

The prototype Magdalen Tower, Churchill

The impressive fountain on the village green in Churchill

reducing the route by about 4 miles. Otherwise, **turn L** (signed Lidstone/Enstone). Follow the road round a sharp right-hand bend (signed Enstone), the small village of Lidstone may be visited by turning left.

Just after the 30 mph signs (Enstone, but not signed) **turn R** at the T-junction (not signed). At the crossroads with the B4022 go straight over (signed Fulwell). On the right-hand corner of this junction stands the Hoar Stone. This is another ancient monument and is what remains of a prehistoric burial chamber. Continue along this road then **turn R** on entering Fulwell (not signed) onto a narrow road alongside farm buildings.

Turn L at the T-junction with the B4022 (signed Charlbury). On a climbing left-hand bend **turn R** (signed Taston/Spelsbury). In Taston **turn L** (signed Taston only). A few yards down this road to your left (before the small green and cross) there is an ancient standing stone in what is now a garden hedge. When you are ready, retrace your steps back to the junction, turning left to follow the sign for Spelsbury. At the staggered crossroads in Spelsbury, **turn L**

(signed Charlbury).

In Charlbury, if you wish to return to the car park, **turn L** into Thames Street (signed Town Centre). **Turn R** at the crossroads with the B4022, following the sign to the Spendlove Centre. The car park is shortly on your right. Otherwise to return to the station, keep straight on until you reach the No Entry signs and **turn R**, following signs back to the station.

• •

CHARLBURY

The town of Charlbury lies in the valley of the River Evenlode, one of the Thames' many tributaries. Today it is a quiet place of pleasant stone cottages and handsome old inns. Not far from the town lies the large estate of Cornbury Park and the remains of the once great hunting forest of Wychwood. For many centuries Charlbury was well known for its glove manufacture, an industry which at its height employed more than 1,000 people. The town's Youth Hostel is a converted glove factory. A friend of mine from the town once told me that in its heyday, there were more than 20 pubs, a fact which sets me wondering how many of Charlbury's gloves had other than the usual number of fingers! For those interested in country crafts, Charlbury has a small museum which preserves many facets of rural life and is open on Sunday afternoons from Easter to October.

Bourton-on-the-Water: A Cotswold Calendar Ride

23 miles

Many a Cotswold calendar could be used as a route sheet for this ride. Despite their popularity, many of the villages remain remarkably unspoilt and exploring them by foot or bike is a real pleasure. The tops of the hills offer wonderful views of English pastoral scenery, while the villages nestled in the valleys offer different pleasures; cottage gardens, golden Cotswold stone, babbling rivers, not to mention the odd cream tea. The ride also passes the Cotswold Farm Park which houses a large collection of rare breeds of farm animal. Bourton-on-the-Water, where the ride starts and finishes, is by far the most commercial of the Cotswold villages, and on summer weekends and bank holidays is often packed to bursting point with trippers. However, it is home to a number of museums and other attractions.

Maps: OS Landranger 163 Cheltenham and Cirencester or OS Touring Map 8 The Cotswolds (GR 167208).

Starting point: The main street in Bourton-on-the-Water which runs alongside the River Windrush. Bourton-on-the-Water is located just off the A429 (Fosse Way) 12 miles east of Cheltenham. There are several large and well-signed car parks in the village. The nearest railway station is Kingham on the London Paddington to Worcester line. If travelling by train, it is probably better to start and finish the ride at Stow-on-the-Wold which is closer to Kingham station.

Refreshments: Food is readily available in Bourton itself and in Stow. We recommend the Mousetrap Inn at Bourton and the Black Horse, Naunton. Light refreshments and lunches are available at the Cotswold Farm Park and teas etc at the Mill Museum in Lower Slaughter and St Edward's Cafe in the Market Square in Stow. Alternatively there are many good spots to have a picnic and on a summer's day the 'stop me and buy one' ice cream tricycles can often be found.

The route: The ride is a challenging one with more or less constant undulations. Despite the popularity of some of the destinations, the roads taken are surprisingly quiet. The route may be shortened, by 3 miles, by cutting out a visit to the hilltop town of Stow-on-the-Wold.

From the car park, make your way to the village centre (by the river) and head out of Bourton upstream with the church on your right.

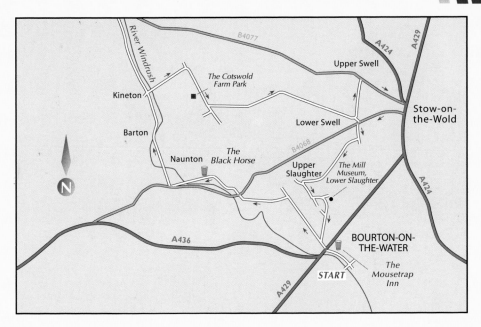

Turn R at the T-junction with the A429 and then **turn L** (signed Naunton/Cotswold Farm Park). Just after passing Manor Farm, **turn L** (signed Lower Harford). To your left there is a lovely view down into the Windrush valley. Soon the road plunges steeply to meet the B4068. Take care as there is gravel on the steep descent. Go straight over at the crossroads with the B4068 (signed Naunton) and ride through Naunton. Climb steadily out and at the B4068 **turn R** (signed Guiting Power/ Winchcombe). **Turn R** (signed Guiting Power/Winchcombe) and ride through Barton to Kineton.

At a staggered crossroads on the far edge of Kineton, **turn R** (not signed). Take care as the road has a poor surface. Descend to cross the River Windrush at the footbridge over the ford. At the next junction, **bear L** uphill (not signed). **Turn R** at the T-junction (signed Farm Park). The Cotswold Farm Park is about ½ mile along this road on the right-hand side. If not visiting the park, continue to the following crossroads and **turn L** (signed Stow/Lower Swell).

Keep straight on for 3½ miles into Lower Swell. If you would like to take the short cut, missing out Stow-on-the-Wold, then **turn R** onto the B4068 and continue at the * below, otherwise **turn L** before the junction with the B4068 (signed Upper Swell). **Turn R** onto the B4077 (signed Upper Swell/ Stow-on-the-Wold). On entering Stow, **turn R** onto the A424 (not signed) and at the traffic lights

Relaxing at the ford, Upper Slaughter

turn **R** onto the A429 (signed Cirencester). **Turn L** immediately (signed Town Centre, High Street) and ride into the Market Square.

When you are ready to leave Stow take Digbeth Street (near the preaching cross on the Market Square) and **turn R** (signed Cirencester/Cheltenham A436). Go straight over at the staggered crossroads with traffic lights (signed Lower Swell/Naunton). In Lower Swell, * **turn L** (signed The Slaughters). **Turn R** (not signed) and on entering Upper Slaughter **turn R** (signed no through road, unsuitable for motors). Cross the ford on the footbridge and ride up the hill. **Turn R** (not signed). **Turn L** at the T-junction (signed Lower Slaughter/Bourton-on-the-Water). **Bear L** (signed Lower Slaughter).

Lower Slaughter is well worth investigating. The Mill Museum and teashop is over the first footbridge. Leave Lower Slaughter by **turning R** opposite the first footbridge over the river (not signed). **Turn L** at the T-junction (signed Bourton-on-the-Water/The Rissingtons) and **turn L** at the next T-junction (signed Bourton-on-the-Water). Take care and **turn R** onto the A429 (signed Cirencester) and soon **turn L** (not signed) and ride back into Bourton-on-the-Water.

• • • • • • • • • • • • • • • • • • • •

BOURTON-ON-THE-WATER

For most tourists, Bourton-on-the-Water

is the archetypal Cotswold village and is therefore a 'must visit' for every coach party or family visiting the area. The result is that the peace and tranquillity which undoubtedly once pervaded it has long fled. However, it offers a wide choice of refreshments and several attractions which may appeal, especially to families. There is the Birdland park and gardens housing birds from all around the world in over 50 aviaries and two tropical glasshouses. There is also a motor museum and a model village.

THE COTSWOLD FARM PARK

The Cotswold Farm Park offers an interesting day out. It is home to over 50 breeding flocks and herds of rare domestic animals; sheep, cattle, pigs, goats, poultry and wildfowl. There is plenty of opportunity to get 'hands on' with the animals in the pets corner and to bottle-feed lambs in the spring. Children can learn to drive mini-tractors on the play farm and there is an audio tour of 'animals through the ages' and demonstrations of various country crafts and skills. If you decide to visit the park on the ride make sure you leave plenty of time because there is a lot to see and do.

The old mill (now a museum) at Lower Slaughter

The park is open daily from 1st April to 1st October from 10.30 am to 5 pm (6 pm Sundays and Bank Holidays). An entrance fee is charged.

Winchcombe: Exploring the Escarpment

18 miles

This ride starts from the picturesque and historic town of Winchcombe, the site of the ancient walled city of Mercia. The route winds its way up to Belas Knap, a Bronze Age long barrow, and returns through wooded country via Hailes with its ruined abbey. Care should be exercised along the very narrow roads as they are popular with horse riders and walkers. Some of the road surfaces are not in the best of conditions and may be slippery. Despite this you get a real feel of being 'in the heart of the countryside' with wonderful views from the high points along the way.

Maps: OS Landranger 163 Cheltenham and Cirencester or OS Touring Map 8 The Cotswolds (GR 022284).

Starting point: This ride starts out from the well-signed long-stay car park (off Back Lane) in Winchcombe, 7 miles north-east of Cheltenham. The full ride is 18 miles long, but a short cut can reduce it to 11 miles, at the cost of missing out on a visit to Hailes Abbey.

Refreshments: The town contains a wide variety of pubs, and tearooms serving both full meals and snacks. On the route there is also a tearoom at the Hailes Fruit Farm. On a clear day why not take a picnic to eat while admiring the views of the Malverns and Wales from Belas Knap or while sitting by the mellow ruins of Hailes Abbey.

The route: This ride involves a substantial and steep climb up the escarpment and also an 'exciting' descent on a narrow and wooded road. We would therefore not classify this as a ride suitable for beginners or families with young children. However, those who rise to the challenge will be amply rewarded with quiet roads and stunning views.

Turn R out of the car park then **turn R** again at the crossroads (signed Cheltenham). At the top of the incline **turn R** at the T-junction (the Museum and Tourist Information Centre stand on the right-hand corner of this junction). **Turn R** along the B4632 towards Cheltenham. **Turn L** (signed Brockhampton/Andoversford) and a little way along this road **turn L again** into Corndean Lane (also signed Brockhampton/ Andoversford).

The road soon starts climbing. Just after a steep left-hand bend you will see some car parking to your

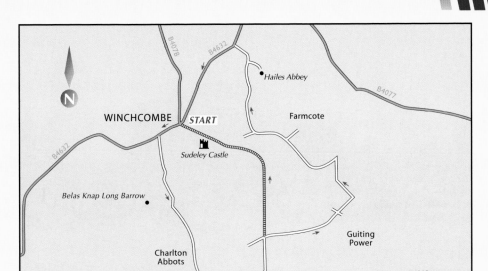

left. Look down into the valley from this point and enjoy the panoramic view of Winchcombe with Sudeley Castle standing out prominently. From here you can visit the ancient long barrow called Belas Knap, parking your bicycle and walking up. It is quite a long way up but well worth the effort.

When you are ready, continue the climb. Go straight over at the crossroads (signed Brockhampton/ Andoversford) and also keep straight on at the next crossroads (signed Sevenhampton/ Andoversford). **Turn L** (signed Sevenhampton Village). Take care as the road down into the village is steep. Cross the ford (there is a little path to the right-hand side if you do not want to risk riding through!) and climb away. **Turn L**

at the T-junction (not signed but road bears sign 'Unsuitable for Motor Vehicles'). Follow this narrow road into Brockhampton. Then go straight over at the crossroads (signed Rodes Memorial Hall).

After a gentle climb out of the village, **turn L** (signed Guiting Power/Winchcombe). **Turn L again** (signed Roel/Winchcombe). You are now riding down the Salt Way which was part of the medieval trackway linking the important salt workings at Droitwich in Worcestershire with the head of the navigable Thames near Lechlade. At the following crossroads you may, if you wish, return directly to Winchcombe by going straight across and following the road steeply downhill and past Sudeley

Hailes Abbey

Castle. Otherwise **turn R** (signed Guiting Power).

After a descent go straight across at the crossroads (signed Kineton, gated road). Soon after the first gate the Manor House will be seen some way off on the left. Keep an eye out for a left-hand turn as it is easy to miss! **Turn L** at the crossroads (not signed but carries a sign 'Unsuitable for Motor Vehicles'). If you come to a ford you have gone too far so turn around and retrace your steps.

Pass through a second gate. Please make sure that the gates are closed where appropriate. At the T-junction **turn L** (not signed). At the next T-junction **turn L** (signed Winchcombe). Near the top of the climb (Sudeley Hill) **turn R** (signed Little Farmcote). The descent starts fairly gently but becomes steeper. With the narrow road and rough edges, care should be taken on the way down. At one point the road appears to fork, **keep left** here as the right arm is a farm entrance! Do take your time and enjoy the views.

Ride through the village of Hailes then on the outskirts **turn sharp R** signed Hailes Fruit Farm to visit Hailes Abbey. After visiting the abbey, retrace your steps to the junction where you turned sharp right and **bear R**. Soon after passing over the railway bridge **turn L** at the T-junction with the

B4632 (signed Winchcombe) and ride back into the town. Follow 'Long Stay Parking' signs to return to the car park.

BELAS KNAP LONG BARROW

Belas Knap is a Neolithic long barrow, some 4,500 years old, built in the same Severn/Cotswold tradition as the Nympsfield Long Barrow and Hetty Peggler's Tump (the Uley Long Barrow). It is situated high up on the Cotswold escarpment enjoying commanding views down to Winchcombe and away towards the west. The impressive false entrance at its northern end was probably designed to detract interest from the true entrances at the sides. Like other Severn/Cotswold long barrows, it has multiple internal chambers, which were found to contain 30 skeletons. Dry-stone walling made from stones quarried at the site was used extensively to support the internal structure, to create the false entrance and to surround the site. This tradition, which contributes so much to the character of the Cotswolds, can therefore be seen to have very ancient roots indeed.

HAILES ABBEY

Hailes Abbey, located at the foot of the escarpment, a few miles north-east of Winchcombe, was founded in 1246 by Richard, Earl of Cornwall following his escape from a shipwreck off the Isles of Scilly. It became an important place of

Winchcombe is full of splendid old buildings

pilgrimage when Richard's son Edmund gave the Abbey a vial containing 'Holy Blood of Christ', confirmed as such by the Pope. Its fame lasted until the Dissolution, when it was reduced to ruins. Now only the cloisters and a few segments of wall remain. However, trees have been planted to help perpetuate the original plan, and there is a museum nearby which houses some of the artefacts found during excavations.

10
Winchcombe: Hills Viewed from Afar

19 miles

From the delightful town of Winchcombe, this is an easy, gentle ride going out through Greet, with its railway station and steam trains, looping around through Beckford, giving you the chance to visit a silk centre and then returning to Winchcombe via Gretton. It gives you ample opportunity to admire both Bredon Hill and the Cotswold escarpments, safe in the knowledge that you will not be climbing them!

Maps: OS Landranger 163 Cheltenham and Cirencester or OS Touring Map 8 The Cotswolds (GR 022284).

Starting point: This ride starts out from the well-signed long-stay car park (off Back Lane) in Winchcombe, some 7 miles north-east of Cheltenham.

Refreshments: The town contains a wide variety of pubs, and tearooms serving both full meals and snacks. Along the route there are pubs at Greet and Gretton and a café at the Silk Centre at Beckford.

The route: This is a pleasant amble through only gently undulating countryside. It is suitable for both families and beginners, although care must be exercised on the two crossings of the A46.

Turn R out of the car park and then go straight over at the crossroads (signed Greet). In Greet follow the B4078 (signed Evesham). Don't be surprised if you hear a train whistle or see and smell steam and coal smoke, because Greet is currently the terminus for the Gloucestershire and Warwickshire Railway, and steam trains often operate between there and Toddington further up the escarpment (for more details, see route 4).

Go straight on at the next crossroads with the B4077 (signed Evesham B4078). **Turn L** (signed Dumbleton) and ride through this interesting village which nestles at the foot of Dumbleton Hill. **Turn R** at the T-junction with the A46 and then after about 100 yards **turn L** (signed Grafton). Take care at these two junctions.

Turn L at the crossroads (signed Beckford). You will pass the Beckford Silk Centre which is open Monday to Saturday 9 am to 5.30 pm. The site contains an open workshop, retail shop, gallery and

48

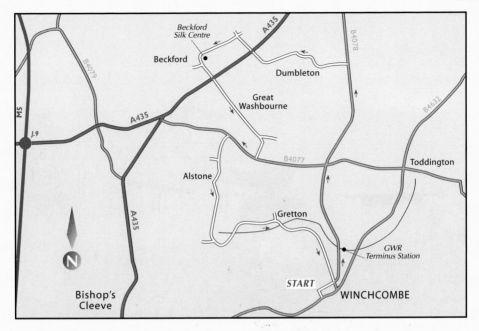

café. **Turn L** at the T-junction (signed Evesham). At the following T-junction with the A46 **turn L** and **immediately turn R** (signed Great Washbourne). Ride though Great Washbourne and on to Alderton. Here **turn R** (signed Tewkesbury). At the T-junction with the B4077 **turn R** (also signed Tewkesbury).

Turn L (signed Alstone). In the village **turn L** (signed Dixton). Ride through Dixton and on to **turn L** at a T-junction (signed Gretton/ Winchcombe). In Gretton **turn R** at the T-junction (signed Winchcombe). Soon after passing the Winchcombe name sign you will pass some older houses and then descend to the crossroads you crossed on the way out. **Turn R** here to return to the car park.

WINCHCOMBE

Today Winchcombe is a beautiful town of mainly 16th and 17th-century Cotswold stone houses. You will find that time spent walking around its roads and lanes (excellent walking guides are available from the Tourist Information Centre) very rewarding. There are two museums (the Folk and Police Museum and the Railway Museum), a pottery and many shops to interest both cyclists and non-cyclists alike. Sudeley Castle and gardens are only a short walk from the town centre.

Winchcombe first came to prominence in the 8th century. It was from there that the Hwicce (a sub-kingdom of Mercia) was ruled, and it even had its own mint. In AD 787 King Offa founded a nunnery, and later King Kenwulf founded an Abbey dedicated to the Archbishop of Canterbury. Later this Abbey was refounded as a Benedictine establishment which, through the Middle Ages, came to dominate the economy of the town to such an extent that when it

Topiary in the churchyard at Alstone

was dissolved in 1539, Winchcombe declined almost into oblivion. The parish church dates from 1460 and each of its 400 gargoyles is supposed to represent a real local character. Once the Abbey had gone, locals had to turn to other ways to make a living, and in the 1620s they explored the economic potential of growing recently introduced tobacco.

This brought them up against powerful people, with vested interests, who succeeded in making tobacco growing illegal in this country to protect their own colonial investments. However, this didn't stop the townsfolk who continued growing tobacco despite occasional armed intervention.

Northleach and the Windrush

20 miles

Northleach used to be a noisy place, but has taken on a much quieter character since the A40 has bypassed it. This is an excellent starting point if not everybody in the family wants to ride. There are two interesting museums and a classic Cotswold Wool Church to explore while the riders are away. For the riders, the route offers a dramatic contrast between the open hills, expansive views and fields full of Cotswold sheep, and the gentle riverside water meadows and willow trees of the Windrush valley.

Maps: OS Landranger 163 Cheltenham and Cirencester or OS Touring Map 8 The Cotswolds (GR 114146).

Starting point: This ride starts in the centre of Northleach (the Market Place) which is located just off the A40, 11 miles south-east of Cheltenham. Car parking is available in the Market Square or at the Cotswold Countryside Collection on the A429.

Refreshments: Food is available in Northleach; we recommend the Corner Green Café and the Red Lion. Light refreshments are available at the Cotswold Countryside Collection located on the A429, just outside Northleach. Along the route we recommend the Fox at Little Barrington. If you prefer eating al fresco, then why not take the opportunity to picnic amid the water-meadows and wild fowl on the Sherborne estate?

The route: The first half of the route involves several steep climbs offering panoramic views of the surrounding area. In contrast, the second half of the route is relatively flat and gentle as it follows the river Windrush back to Northleach.

From the Market Place, join the main street by **turning R** and heading in an easterly direction. **Turn L** (signed Farmington, Farmington Road). The climb from the junction is quite steep. Soon after passing under the A40 the road descends very steeply followed by a steep climb out (take care!).

Turn R at the T-junction (signed Farmington/Bourton-on-the-Water). In Farmington **turn L** (signed Stow-on-the-Wold/Bourton-on-the-Water). After a long undulating climb **turn R** at a T-junction (signed Clapton/Sherborne). At the top of a further climb **turn L** (signed Clapton-on-the-Hill). Enjoy the marvellous

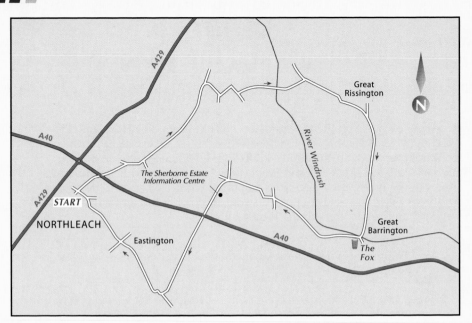

views as you ride along this road, you will feel as though you are on the roof of the Cotswolds. At the T-junction **turn R** (signed Sherborne). If you want to explore the village, take the left turn (no through road).

Soon **turn L** (not signed but 'Unsuitable for Motors'). This road descends steeply and for a long distance. It is very narrow so care is needed but traffic is minimal. At the end, **turn R** at the T-junction (not signed). Ride into Great Rissington. In the village follow signs for The Barringtons/Burford. Just after the Lamb Inn **turn R** to visit the church, and also to see the picturesque driveway leading to the manor house alongside the church.

After visiting the church return to

the junction near the Lamb and **turn R** again following signs for The Barringtons/Burford. **Turn R** at the T-junction (signed The Barringtons/Burford). The road to Great Barrington is largely a gentle downhill run. Just after the Great Barrington village sign pause at the wrought-iron gates and peer into the deer park. There are often deer to be seen, sometimes at close quarters.

At the junction in the village **bear R** (signed Little Barrington), passing the war memorial on the left. On a left-hand bend, **turn R** (signed Windrush/Sherborne). On your left stands the Fox Inn. In Windrush **bear R** (signed Sherborne). Go straight on at the first junction in Sherborne, then **turn L** (signed Farmington/

The village green in spring, Farmington

Northleach). Enjoy the views into the valley on your right. **Turn L** at the crossroads (signed Northleach/Oxford).

Near the top of the climb and on the left is the entrance to the Ewepen car park and information centre which is part of the Sherborne Park Estate. The information centre is worth a look at. Through the barn is a low building with some benches to sit on. After the visit return to the road and **turn L** and continue the gentle climb.

Go straight over at the crossroads with the A40 (not signed). This narrow road gives you another long gentle descent. Near the end is another National Trust property, Lodge Park. Admission is by advanced booking only, but you can see the buildings from the road. **Turn R** at the T-junction (signed Eastington/Northleach). Almost as soon as you join this road it descends very steeply with some twists and turns followed by a steep climb out. Go straight on at the next junction. Stay on the 'main road' and 'weave' your way across the staggered crossroads following signs for Northleach. Just after Northleach comes into view there is another steep descent. At the T-junction **turn L** (signed Stow-on-the-Wold/Cheltenham) and ride back into the town centre.

NORTHLEACH

In the Middle Ages, Northleach was one of the most important wool trading centres in the Cotswolds, and it has a magnificent parish church paid for by the profits of the trade. However, as with all places it had its troublemakers, and in the late 18th century the philanthropist and prison reformer Sir George Onesiphorus Paul built a 'House of Correction' on the Fosse Way (present A429) just to the west of the village. Today this building has been imaginatively converted into a museum of rural life, the Cotswold Countryside Collection. You can not only visit the restored 18th-century cells and the Victorian court house, but discover all about life in the Cotswolds of the past. Alternatively, for those of a more musical disposition, why not visit Keith Harding's World of Mechanical Music at Oak House in the High Street?

SHERBORNE

This delightful village on the banks of the Sherborne Brook (a tributary of the River Windrush) has been part of the Sherborne House Estate for many centuries. At one time the estate was owned by the Abbots of Winchcombe. Each May, their many thousands of sheep were driven from the sheep runs on the wolds to the estate for shearing, a practice which gave much needed (though temporary) employment to the locals. After the Dissolution, the estate passed to the Dutton family and it was eventually left to the National Trust. It is a lovely place for a picnic, and there is a nature trail and many way marked walks.

The village post office, Sherborne

Visiting the Rural Romans

20 miles

The main attraction on this ride from Northleach is the splendid Roman villa at Chedworth. This is looked after by the National Trust and is well worth a visit. At the villa there is an information centre/gift shop, and a small lecture theatre where you can watch a video introduction to Chedworth. After the villa the route passes through Withington. A steep long climb leads to Chedworth village. The hills then become less severe as the route winds its way down to the Roman road at Fosse Cross before turning back to Northleach via the delightful Coln valley.

Maps: OS Landranger 163 Cheltenham and Cirencester or OS Touring Map 8 The Cotswolds (GR 114146).

Starting point: This ride starts in the centre of Northleach (the Market Place) which is located just off the A40, 11 miles south-east of Cheltenham. Car parking is available in the Market Square.

Refreshments: Food is available in Northleach. We recommend the Corner Green Café and the Red Lion. Light refreshments are also available at the Cotswold Museum of Rural Life located on the A429, just outside Northleach.

The route: This ride is moderately hilly with a couple of steep climbs, especially in the first half.

From the Market Place in Northleach, go to the top left-hand corner (towards the church) and ride along a narrow road passing a bakery on the left. At the T-junction **turn R** (not signed). **Turn L** at the next T-junction (also not signed). **Turn R** (signed Yanworth/Roman Villa). Note the amusing road name, All Alone. Go straight on at the crossroads with the A429 (signed Yanworth/Roman Villa), and also go straight on at the next crossroads (signed Yanworth/

Roman Villa). In Yanworth **turn L** (signed Roman Villa).

When you reach the villa junction, if you want to visit the villa, go straight ahead (signed Roman Villa Only). Afterwards, return to the junction and **turn L** (signed Withington). If not visiting the villa, **turn R** (signed Withington). Go straight over at the crossroads (signed Withington). In Withington, and soon after passing the King's Head, **turn L** (signed

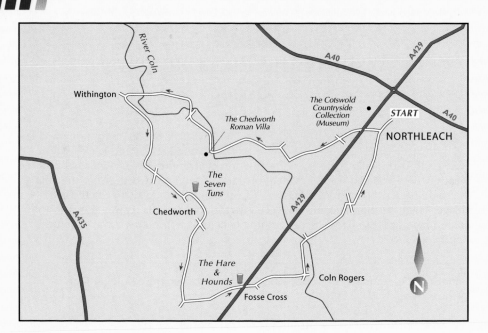

Andoversford/Cheltenham). Follow this road through the village then soon after passing the Mill Inn **turn L** (signed Chedworth) and **keep L** at the next junction by staying on the 'main road' (signed Chedworth).

After a long, hard but rewarding climb **bear L** (signed Chedworth) and soon go straight over at the crossroads (signed Chedworth). **Bear L** (signed Chedworth) and ride into the village. After a steep descent **bear R** (signed Lower Chedworth/Calmsden), passing the Seven Tuns pub a short distance off to the left. **Turn R** (signed Calmsden). Go straight on at the crossroads (signed Calmsden). At the T-junction (with a grass triangle in the middle) **turn L** (signed Fossebridge/Northleach).

At the T-junction with the A429 **turn L** (signed Stow). Within a very short distance **turn R** (signed Coln Rogers/Bibury). Take care at these two junctions. The Hare and Hounds is opposite the Coln Rogers turning. Soon **turn L** (signed Coln Rogers). In the village **turn L** at the crossroads (signed Coln St Dennis/ Fossebridge). This signpost is on the right at the junction and can be partly obscured by vegetation. Should you wish to visit the Saxon church go straight on instead.

In Coln St Dennis **turn R** (signed Calcot/Northleach). **Turn L** (signed Northleach) and climb out of the village. At the crossroads, go straight on (signed Northleach). In Northleach **turn R** at the T-junction with Church Walk (signed Town Centre). **Turn L** at

The Chedworth Roman Villa

the next T-junction (not signed). **Turn L** again and follow the narrow street back into the Market Place.

• •

CHEDWORTH ROMAN VILLA

It wasn't just Romans that lived in Roman villas, or so you discover when you visit the Chedworth Roman Villa. Many in the upper levels of Iron Age society readily adopted the Roman way of life and did very well out of the improved opportunities for trade brought about by the stability and transport links the Romans rapidly established. This villa with over a mile of walls, several bath houses, central heating, living rooms, water shrine, kitchens, farm buildings etc was owned by a rich Romano-British family and is one of the largest in the country. The site, located in a secluded wooded valley, was initially excavated in 1874, and over the years has yielded a vivid insight into life in rural Roman Britain.

The Burgesses of Burford

13 miles

Burford's main street is built on a hill and the River Windrush meanders its way through the lowest part of town. The ride follows this delightful river as it winds its way through water-meadows to the east of Burford. You pass through tiny Widford with its isolated church built on top of a Roman villa and then continue climbing briefly away from the river before returning to meet the river at the lovely village of Swinbrook.

Maps: OS Landranger 163 Cheltenham and Cirencester and 164 Oxford, Chipping Norton and Bicester (GR 254123).

Starting point: This ride starts from the free car park at the lower end of Burford. This is accessed from the main street by following the parking signs into Church Lane. Burford is a popular destination, and the car park may get full at busy times.

Refreshments: The town contains a wide variety of pubs, restaurants, hotels and tearooms. We recommend the Priory Tearooms and the Mermaid Inn, both of which are located on the main street. Food may also be found on the route at the Maytime Inn in Asthall or the Swan in Swinbrook.

The route: The ride climbs and falls regularly to and from river level, but the climbs are neither steep nor long. The longest is up a delightful wooded valley between Fordwells and Swinbrook. If desired, some of the climb may be avoided by taking the direct road from Fordwells to Swinbrook.

From the car park entrance **turn L**, and **turn L again** at the T-junction. Ride out of Burford then **turn L** (signed Widford/Swinbrook). Widford is the first village along the route. To visit St Oswald's church **turn L** by Widford Mill Farm. A short distance along this road the footpath leads off to the right. Please leave your bicycle here and walk to the church.

Afterwards, retrace your steps to Widford Mill Farm and **turn L**. At the crossroads keep straight on (signed Asthall) passing the Swinbrook cricket ground on your left. Just after the climb into Asthall, and immediately in front of a straight avenue of trees **turn L** (not signed) into the heart of the village. Along this road you will pass the Maytime Inn on your left. **Turn L** at the T-junction (not signed). The road crosses the Windrush on a stone bridge. Soon

Sheep grazing by Widford church

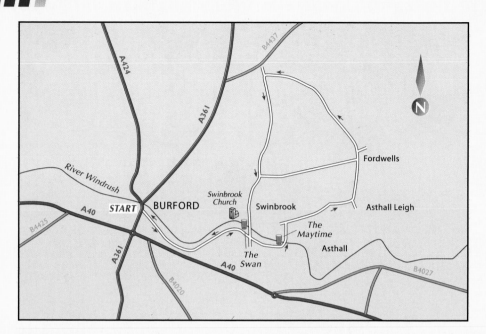

the road climbs and is very narrow. At the top of the climb **turn R** at the T-junction (signed Asthall Leigh).

Ride into Asthall Leigh and **bear L** (signed Fordwells/Leafield). Before you get to Fordwells there is a steep descent so take care. In the village a short cut may be taken by turning left (signed Swinbrook) and left again at the following T-junction into Swinbrook, otherwise carry straight on.

At the next junction **bear L** (signed Shipton-under-Wychwood). Take time to pause and look at the trough on your left which used to be the village water supply. Ride out and along the pleasant valley before gently climbing. At the T-junction **turn L** (signed

Swinbrook). There is now a gentle descent into Swinbrook. Near the bottom, on a left turn, there are some houses, and opposite, a pond with ducks and geese. There is a lane off to the right which runs alongside the pond. So if you want to pause and feed some ducks turn right into the lane, otherwise keep straight on. Soon afterwards **bear R** (signed Swinbrook/Burford). If you took the earlier short cut, rejoin the main route here by **turning L**.

Keep on the road through the village. The church is on your right as is, a little further along, the Swan public house. Soon the road recrosses the Windrush. At the crossroads **turn R** (signed Widford/Burford). Ride through Widford then **turn R** at the T-junction (signed Burford). In

One of the more unusual inhabitants of Burford

Burford **turn R** into the street named Guildenford. **Turn R** into the car park and the end of the ride.

● ● ● ● ● ● ● ● ● ● ● ● ● ● ● ● ● ● ● ●

BURFORD

Burford's history is dominated by the trade in wool and hides which, in the Middle Ages, made some of its merchants very rich men. They endowed Burford with some magnificent buildings (for example the huge parish church and the Great House) and some illustrating their sense of social responsibility (almshouses and a school). Local government was in the hands of Burgesses who levied tolls to trade, operated the petty law court, made by-laws and assessed the townsfolk for taxes. The Burgesses' Roll, which sets this out is on view in the Tolsey (the place where trade tolls were collected) now an interesting museum. These rights didn't go down well with Sir Lawrence Tanfield who bought the manor in 1617. He was a lawyer, and Chief Baron to the Exchequer to boot, and sued the Burgesses, proving that their long-practised rights were illegal. Presumably he then pocketed the tolls and fines himself. When he died, he was so unpopular, he was buried at midnight! Burford achieved notoriety during the Civil War when a group of army levellers were pursued into the cellar of the Crown Inn (now a pharmacy) and some were killed.

WIDFORD CHURCH

The tiny church in the hamlet of Widford stands alone on a plateau above the River Windrush. It was built on the site of a Roman villa. There is a mosaic floor underneath the chancel (no longer visible due to souvenir hunters). The church dates from the 13th century and there are fragments of 14th-century wall paintings. Unusually, the early 19th-century box pews are intact. They are so tall that there is no chance of being seen by your neighbour; only the vicar, high up in his Jacobean pulpit, could see which of his congregation had dropped off during the sermon!

SWINBROOK

The church in the village of Swinbrook contains two marvellous triple-decker marble tombs of six members of the Fettiplace family who once owned a large mansion between the church and the river. They are depicted lying, rather suavely, on their sides and propped up on one elbow. The costumes are exquisitely carved and it is interesting to follow them forward in time from the 16th through to the mid-17th century. The churchyard contains some excellent examples of 'bale' tombs and also the graves of Unity and Nancy Mitford whose childhood years in Swinbrook House are described in Jessica Mitford's book *Hons and Rebels*.

14

Bibury and the Coln Valley: Trout for Tea?

17 miles

Bibury is a great favourite with visitors to the Cotswolds, and contains what is probably the most photographed group of cottages in the world, Arlington Row. There is also a museum and a fish farm where you can catch a trout for lunch or simply buy one already prepared for cooking. The crystal clear River Coln runs through the middle of the village. The ride proceeds through Coln St Aldwyns and Quenington before looping round to Ready Token. Nobody seems to know just why it is so called although there are plenty of theories! Then on to the most westerly point of the ride at Barnsley where gardens may be visited. The route continues to Coln Rogers and down the beautiful Coln valley to Bibury.

Maps: OS Landranger 163 Cheltenham and Cirencester or OS Touring Map 8 The Cotswolds (GR 115059).

Starting point: The ride starts from outside the Swan Hotel in the centre of Bibury, 6 miles north-east of Cirencester. Free parking is available in a car park immediately west of the main street, near where it crosses the River Coln and opposite the museum and trout farm.

Refreshments: Bibury has several places serving food. We recommend the Jenny Wren tearooms at the eastern end of the main street, and the Catherine Wheel public house at the western end.

The route: The ride is undulating, but there are no really big hills. However, there are one or two short, sharp climbs and some long, gentle descents.

From the Swan Hotel, head east along the B4425 (signed Aldsworth/Burford). On a climbing left-hand bend **turn R** (signed Coln St Aldwyns). Climb out of the village. This is not a difficult climb but it is longish, take time on the way up to look back at Bibury nestling in the valley.

At the T-junction (with a grass triangle in the middle) **turn R** (signed Coln St Aldwyns/Fairford). Ride into Coln St Aldwyns. Go straight on at the crossroads (signed Quenington) passing the post-office on the right. Climb out of Coln St Aldwyns and into Quenington. Go straight on at the crossroads (Springfield Road). At the crossroads, **turn R** (signed Ampney St Peter/Cirencester). Ride

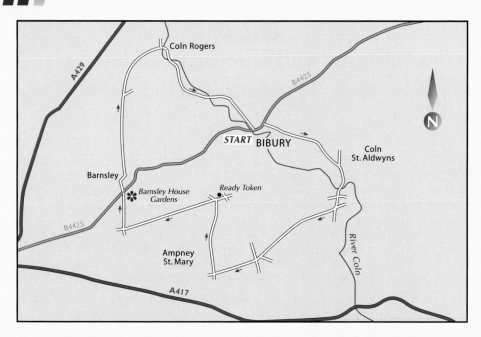

out of Quenington. At a junction of five roads (in the hamlet of Sunhill) go straight on (signed Ampney St Peter/Cirencester). **Turn R** at the crossroads (signed Ready Token/Bibury). At the next crossroads (Ready Token itself), **turn L** (signed Barnsley/ Cirencester.) This stretch of road is part of the Roman road, Akeman street. **Turn R** at the crossroads, this small road is not signed although the other roads are. At the crossroads with the B4425, at the edge of Barnsley, if visiting the gardens **turn R** into the village and follow the signs guiding you in, then afterwards, return to the crossroads and **turn R** (signed Coln Rogers). Otherwise go straight on (signed Coln Rogers).

Keep straight on at the small, unsigned crossroads and follow the road out of Barnsley. At the first junction after leaving the village keep straight on (signed Coln Rogers). At the crossroads go straight over (signed Coln Rogers). After a steep descent into the village, **turn R** at the T-junction (signed Winson/Bibury). At the T-junction **turn L** (signed Ablington/ Winson). In Winson follow the 'main road' through the village. Ride out of Winson and **turn L** (signed Ablington/Bibury). Ride into Ablington then **turn R** (signed Bibury). Follow this road back into Bibury passing the trout farm on the right.

The River Coln

BIBURY

Bibury is a delightful village although William Morris' description of it as 'the most beautiful village in the Cotswolds' has over the years guaranteed it more than its fair share of visitors. If you can, visit it midweek, when you will be able to appreciate its charms in more peace. The River Coln, which runs through its centre, was once used to wash the cloth produced by local weavers. This cloth was hung up to dry on the aptly named Rack Isle, between the river and Arlington Row. Take some time to explore the back lanes and the delightful 13th-century church. You cannot help but notice the large number of trout in the river, and next to the bridge and the Swan Hotel there is a trout-farm where you can watch the fish being fed, and even choose one for supper! The nearby Arlington Mill Museum is well worth a visit. It not only houses interesting displays about the history of Bibury, it also contains many beautiful examples of furniture and furnishings from members of the Arts and Crafts movement inspired by William Morris.

BARNSLEY HOUSE GARDENS

These Arts and Crafts style gardens are the work of the well-known garden designer Rosemary Verey who has owned the William and Mary manor house since the 1960s. The 4½ acre gardens are densely planted in the Gertrude Jekyll style and feature a lime walk, a lily pond and a wonderful ornamental vegetable garden. The gardens are open from 1st February to 16th December on Mondays, Wednesdays, Thursdays and Saturdays 10 am to 5.30 pm. An entrance fee is charged.

On the open road

15

Cirencester, Roman Capital of the Cotswolds

22 miles

This delightful ride starts and finishes in Cirencester and explores the Churn and Frome valleys which include some of the Cotswolds' prettiest and least well-known villages. Investigate the Saxon church at Duntisbourne Rouse or the fords at Duntisbourne Leer. The Edwin Lutyens-inspired 'Arts and Crafts' gardens at Misarden Park are less than ½ mile off the route, near Miserden, and at Daneway, the disused Severn and Thames canal can be explored and the restored western portal visited.

Maps: OS Landranger 163 Cheltenham and Cirencester or OS Touring Map 8 The Cotswolds (GR 024020).

Starting point: The ride starts from the Market Place in the centre of Cirencester. Arrivals by car are recommended to park in the Beeches Car Park on Beeches Road. To reach it, drive to the roundabout north-east of the town centre, where the A417, A419 and A429 meet. Take the turning signed Town Centre (London Road). Beeches Road is on your left.

Refreshments: Cirencester contains a variety of pubs, restaurants, and tearooms. For drinks and light lunches, we recommend the restaurant in the Brewery Arts Centre (off Cricklade Street) and the Swan Cafe in Swan Yard (off West Market Place). Around the route, food is available at the Carpenter's Arms, Miserden, the Daneway Inn, Daneway, and the Bell, Sapperton.

The route: The first half of the route is hilly and there are steep climbs out of both the Churn and Frome valleys. The road to Duntisbourne Abbots is one of our favourites in the Cotswolds and is undulating and twisty with wonderful views into a peaceful valley. There is a long descent and one significant climb between Daneway and Sapperton.

To reach the Market Place from the car park, **turn L** out of Beeches Road onto London Road. Go straight across at the traffic-lights (Lewis Lane). **Turn R** (South Way) and **turn R** (North Way). Finally **turn L** into the Market Place.

From the Market Place ride down West Market Place and **bear R** down Spitalgate (signed Gloucester/Cheltenham). At the junction with the A435 (Abbey Way) go straight across (The Whiteway). After 1½ miles, **turn L** (signed Baunton) and

67

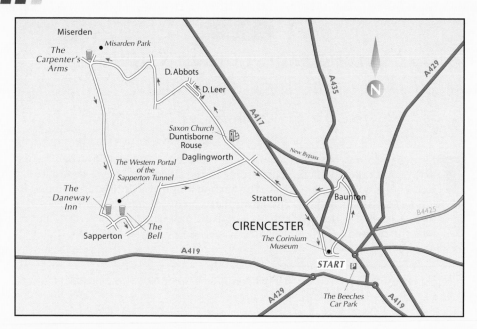

descend with care into the village, crossing the River Churn and climbing sharply to the T-junction with the A435. **Turn R** and immediately **turn L** (not signed, Baunton Lane). At the T-junction with the A417, **turn R** (not signed) and soon **turn L** (signed Daglingworth/Itlay/Park Corner) and ride into Daglingworth. **Turn R** (signed Duntisbournes). After almost a mile, look out for a lychgate on your right leading to the Saxon church of St Michael, Duntisbourne Rouse which is worth exploring.

After another mile **turn R** (signed Duntisbourne Leer). **Turn L** in the village (signed Unsuitable for Motor Vehicles). The reason for this is soon apparent as you encounter a seriously long and

deep ford! Take the path to its left and ride up to the T-junction. **Turn L** (not signed) and climb into Duntisbourne Abbots. **Turn L** at the T-junction (signed Duntisbourne Leer/Winstone/ Sapperton) and soon **bear L** (signed Duntisbourne Leer/Sapperton). Keep on this road following signs to Sapperton until you reach a T-junction. Here **turn R** (signed Winstone/Cheltenham). **Turn L** (signed Miserden) and descend down a pleasantly winding valley to cross the River Frome before climbing out to a road junction. Should you wish to visit Misarden Park, which is well signed from the village centre, or Miserden village (very scenic and with a good pub) take the road behind, to your right.

Otherwise **turn L** (signed

The Market Place, Cirencester

Edgeworth). After 3½ miles descent you will arrive in Daneway. If you want to visit the tunnel portal take the path by the bridge which runs parallel to the pub garden. The portal is about a ten minute walk away, and the pub does cream teas on summer afternoons!

When you are ready to continue, cross the canal bridge and climb the hill to Sapperton. **Turn L** (signed Sapperton Village). At this point the canal tunnel is directly beneath you. Ride through Sapperton and **turn L** at the T-junction (signed Daglingworth/ Duntisbourne). **Turn R** (signed Daglingworth/Cirencester). Follow

the road down into and through Daglingworth and continue back on the road you came out on till the junction with the A417. **Turn R** (with care) onto the A417 (signed Cirencester). After less than ½ mile there is a cycle track on the right side of the road. Recross the road and join this track (signed Town Centre). Follow it as the road it is next to forks right, away from the A-road. Shortly before a no-cycling notice, **turn R** onto a riverside cycle track. Cross the river on a wooden bridge, and soon cross a minor road continuing on the track between two walls. As you approach the centre of Cirencester watch out for pedestrians. At the

The western portal of the Sapperton Tunnel

end of the track, **turn R** onto Park Street and then **turn L** (Black Jack Street) and finally **turn R** (West Market Place) to return to the Market Place.

To return to the car park from the Market Place, ride along the Market Place away from the town centre. Follow the one-way signs. Go straight across at the traffic lights (London Road) and **turn R** (Beeches Road).

● ●

CIRENCESTER

Cirencester of Corinium Dobbunorum was founded as a regional centre for the Dobunni tribe, as a replacement for their fortified town or oppidum believed to have been located at nearby Bagendon.

The town must have been impressive in its heyday with a huge amphitheatre outside the walls (the remains of which can still be visited), baths and a forum. After a lull in its fortunes immediately after the retreat of the Roman armies in the early 5th century, it was re-established in the 8th century as an Anglo-Saxon town and continued to flourish as a medieval centre of the wool trade.

The internationally renowned Corinium Museum displays finds from the town itself and surrounding country villas including several large mosaic floors. It gives an excellent picture of life in Roman Britain and also brings the history of the Cotswolds, from the Neolithic through to the Civil War, to life. It is open Monday to Saturday 10 am to 5 pm and Sundays 2 pm to 5 pm. An entrance fee is charged.

THE SAPPERTON TUNNEL

At 3,808 yards (2¼ miles) long, the Sapperton Tunnel was the longest canal tunnel built when it was completed in 1789 after three years' construction. It completed the Severn & Thames canal linking Stroud with the Thames near Lechlade, a distance of 28¾ miles. Unfortunately it suffered from constant technical problems. The contractor, one Charles Jones, was often too drunk to supervise the work and the tunnel and nearby locks suffered from shoddy workmanship. Also, leakage was an acute problem. Up to 3 million gallons per day were lost through the porous Cotswold limestone. From the gothic Daneway portal the bargemen took anything up to five hours to emerge at the more elaborate eastern portal, which was originally decorated with large statues of Old Father Thames and Madam Sabrina (whoever she was!). The canal was finally abandoned in 1927 and is currently the subject of restoration.

MISARDEN PARK GARDENS

Misarden Park (near Miserden) consists of a mainly 17th-century house (not open), and 20th-century gardens inspired by the Cotswold-based Arts and Crafts movement. The renowned architect Edwin Lutyens contributed to the design of the gardens which may be viewed from April to September on Tuesdays, Wednesdays, and Thursdays (9.30 am to 4.30 pm). An entrance fee is charged for adults.

16

Stroud and *Cider with Rosie*

14 miles

From Stroud the route climbs out of the town onto the high ground to the north-east. It then turns west crossing the Slad Valley to enter Painswick where, with a 1½ mile detour, you can visit the unique Rococo gardens and magnificent churchyard. There is a sharp descent and steep climb up to Bull's Cross before you get the reward of a wonderful 4 mile descent back into Stroud along the Slad valley, made famous by the author Laurie Lee in his book *Cider with Rosie*.

Maps: OS Landranger 163 Cheltenham and Cirencester and 162 Gloucester and Forest of Dean area. Alternatively the entire route is on OS Touring Map 8 The Cotswolds (GR 850051).

Starting point: Stroud is located on the A419, some 12 miles west of Cirencester. Alternatively, it can be approached from north or south along the A46. It may also be reached by train by Great Western Services between Paddington, Swindon and Cheltenham. The ride starts from outside the railway station. Long-term parking is available in a multi-storey car park accessed from the A46, just south of the station.

Refreshments: Stroud is a busy little town, and there are plenty of eating places in the central area. High Street, Withey's Yard (off the High Street) and The Shambles (also near High Street) are the most promising areas for cafés. We can certainly recommend the cakes in Mills Café and Bar in Withey's Yard. Along the route the Butcher's Arms in Sheepscombe (about ½ mile from the route) combines good food with breathtaking views. Painswick has several pubs and light lunches and other refreshments are available at the Painswick Rococo Gardens.

The route: This is one of the most challenging rides in the book and, because of the number of climbs and the steep and twisting descents, it is not suitable for families or inexperienced riders. Having said this, the route offers some truly amazing views and challenging cycling and you will feel a real sense of achievement on its completion.

Go straight across from the station. The road to the right (Russell Street) is one-way, so get off and push your bike (the Shunters pub is on your left). Pass the memorial and Tourist Information Centre on your left and cross the road at the pedestrian lights. Get on your bike

Relaxing in Sheepscombe

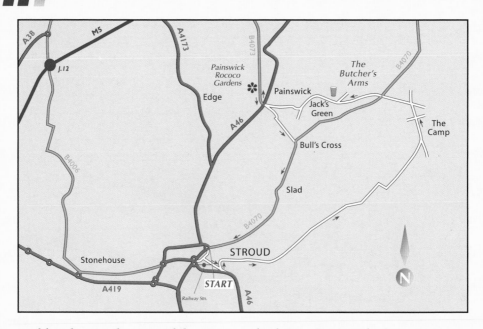

and head towards a roundabout. **Turn L** (signed Bisley, Cornhill) and start climbing. After about ¾ mile you will leave Stroud behind you. The views back are breathtaking. Keep on this road for 3½ miles. Then **turn L** (signed The Camp/Birdlip, Stancombe Lane). At the T-junction, **turn L** (signed The Camp/Birdlip). Cycle through The Camp and then **turn L** (signed Sheepscombe). Go straight over at the crossroads with the B4070 (signed Sheepscombe) and **bear L** (signed Cockshoot/Painswick).

Ride into Jack's Green. If you wish to detour into Sheepscombe look out for right-hand turns down into the village. Otherwise on the exit from Jack's Green **turn R** (signed Painswick). Painswick can be seen ahead and to your right on the other side of the valley. Descend and then

climb into Painswick. On entering the village **turn R** (not signed) and follow the road to the junction with the A46. **Turn L** (not signed).

If you wish to visit the Rococo gardens then **turn R** just beyond the traffic-lights (B4073, signed Gloucester/Rococo Gardens). **Turn L** at the T-junction (not signed). The entrance to the gardens is ¼ mile on the left. On leaving the gardens **turn R** back onto the B-road and follow the one-way system back to the T-junction with the A46, **turn R** and return to the traffic-lights.

If not visiting the gardens, or on leaving them, **turn L** off the A46 after passing the traffic-lights (Bisley Street) and soon **turn R** (Friday Street). The church with its magnificent churchyard is straight

The Red House at Painswick Rococo Gardens

ahead of you should you wish to visit it. Otherwise **turn L** (signed Bull's Cross/Slad, Tibbiwell Lane). This road plunges steeply, care should be taken. It then climbs to a T-junction. **Turn L** here (signed Bull's Cross). At the T-junction with the B4070, **turn R** (not signed). Follow this road down through Slad and back into Stroud. At the T-junction in Stroud, **turn L** (Gloucester Street). At crossroads **turn R** and push your bike through the pedestrian zone following the blue signs to the railway station.

• •

STROUD

As you will soon find out as you try and leave Stroud, as the song says 'the only way is up'! Stroud lies at the meeting place of five steep valleys, and the eastern boundary of the town is 630 feet above the western boundary, even though the two are only 2½ miles apart! Its geographical position with ready access to sheep fleeces, water to power mills, and minerals for dyeing, led it to become the centre of the British cloth industry. At its height, there were over 150 mills in the area, and cloths such as Uley Blue and Stroudwater Scarlet were used all over the world in military uniforms and high-class civilian clothing. Today there are only a couple of mills left. However, the felt which adorns the snooker tables of The Crucible and the tennis balls of Wimbledon are both still made here. The town centre is readily explored on foot and the 56 acre Stratford Park, about ½ mile from the centre, with its arboretum, lake, miniature railway and museum is a pleasant place to relax in.

PAINSWICK

Painswick, located on a high spur of land between two valleys, is a pleasant place to explore on foot. Many of the houses, made from locally-quarried creamy-white stone, are decorated with delightful architectural details. The most famous feature is the churchyard with its vast collection of 18th-century table tombs and magnificent clipped yew trees. Legend has it that only 99 will grow at any one time, the devil taking the hundredth. They have grown so intertwined that it is now difficult to count them. Every year, on or soon after the 19th September, there is a special clipping ceremony during which the parishioners join hands, encircling the church and sing the 'clipping hymn'.

About ¾ mile from the centre of the village lie the Painswick Rococo Gardens which have been lovingly restored to their mid-18th-century glory over the last 15 years. The restoration was inspired by a painting of the gardens in their heyday by Thomas Robins in 1748. The Rococo style of gardening, which refers to the incorporation of natural shapes, balancing asymmetry with formality, was popular for only a short time, and these gardens are unique in this country. They are open from the second Wednesday in January to the 30th November, Wednesday to Sunday plus Bank Holiday Mondays from 11 am to 5 pm. An entrance fee is charged.

Clipped yews and table tombs in Painswick churchyard

17

Nailsworth, Mills and Hills

14 miles

The ride starts by following a cycle track along the disused railway between Nailsworth and Stonehouse which passes numerous cloth mills. Leave the cycle track in Stonehouse and ride through the valley village of Frocester before climbing up the escarpment. At the top you can relax at the Coaley Peak picnic site and enjoy wonderful views of Cam Long Down, the Tyndale Monument and the River Severn. From here you can visit Woodchester Park, or when open the spectacular Woodchester Mansion. Otherwise coast back down to Nailsworth passing by its most recent landmark, a huge wind turbine.

Map: OS Landranger 162 Gloucester and Forest of Dean area (GR 849999).

Starting point: This ride starts from the Egypt Mill car park (patrons only) which is located on the east side of the A46 just north of the centre of Nailsworth. Free long-term parking is available opposite the bus station off the Old Market. To find it, proceed along the A46 to the mini-roundabout on the northern edge of Nailsworth. Turn up Spring Hill and soon turn left into the Old Market. The parking is well signed to your right.

Refreshments: Nailsworth has several cafés and pubs which serve food, and Egypt Mill itself is now a restaurant. There are not too many possibilities for food along the route. On a nice day why not bring a picnic to eat at the Coaley Peak picnic site?

The route: About three quarters of this ride is downhill. The reason for this becomes apparent as you arrive at Frocester and see the escarpment ahead! Don't let this put you off. Although the climb is a long one, take it steady and admire the views unfolding as you ascend. The descent back into Nailsworth gives you a good overview of the topology of the Stroud valleys as well as being a lot of fun!

To get to the starting point from the car park, return to the mini-roundabout and **turn L** up the A46. The entrance to Egypt Mill is almost immediately on your right.

From the Egypt Mill car park join the Stroud Valleys Pedestrian/Cycle Trail by passing through wooden barriers at the north end of the car park. Keep following the blue cycle track signs for Stonehouse. After about 3½ miles, and shortly after passing through a section of tunnel, cross the A419 at a toucan crossing. The impressive Ebley Mill

The River Severn from Frocester Hill

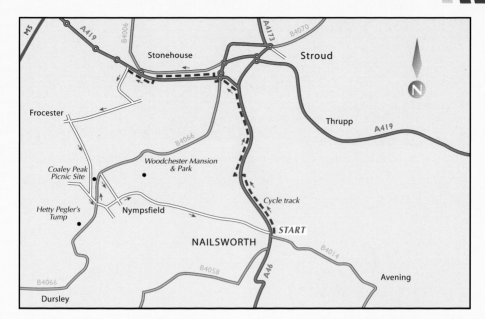

can be seen to your right through the trees. The track runs by the A-road and recrosses it at pedestrian lights some 1 mile further on.

Keep following the signs for Stonehouse and soon, as you approach a roundabout, the track splits. **Bear L** and cross the Stroudwater Canal. The path re-emerges next to a road. Follow and soon **turn L** onto Downton Road (signed Leonard Stanley/Stanley Downton) and cross the canal again.

Ride into Stanley Downton and **turn R** (signed Frocester). **Turn R** at the T-junction (signed Frocester). You should be able to see the high ground of the Forest of Dean to your right. At the junction in Frocester **turn L** (signed Nympsfield/Tetbury). The road

soon starts to climb up the escarpment. At the T-junction at the top **turn L** (signed Selsley/ Stroud, B4066). The Coaley Peak picnic area is ¼ mile on your left with the Nympsfield long barrow near its entrance. However, if you would like to make a short detour to visit the Uley long barrow (also known as Hetty Pegler's Tump) **turn R** instead. The barrow is ¼ mile on your right.

When you are ready to continue, return to the B4066 and **turn L** out of the picnic site and shortly **turn R** (signed Woodchester Park/ Nympsfield). The entrance to Woodchester Park (NT) is on your left. At the junction in Nympsfield, **turn L** (signed Nailsworth). Descend into Nailsworth, passing the wind turbine as you go. You will emerge in Spring Hill,

Nympsfield long barrow

Nailsworth. **Turn R** immediately before the roundabout at the bottom to return to the long-stay parking or **turn L** at the roundabout (signed A46 Stroud) and almost immediately **turn R** to return to Egypt Mill.

● ●

THE STROUD VALLEYS PEDESTRIAN/CYCLE TRAIL

The trail was the idea of a local resident in response to a competition organised in 1981 by the local Quakers to find a job creation scheme that would be of real benefit to the community. Construction along the route of the disused Stonehouse to Nailsworth railway line was begun in 1982, and the final section opened in 1986. The trail is not only a rich wildlife corridor, it also passes many

old and restored woollen mills including Egypt Mill, whose water wheel still turns in the bar. The Stonehouse & Nailsworth Railway Company was formed by Act of Parliament in 1863 and the railway opened in 1867. However, the construction proved more difficult and expensive than originally thought, and within ten months the company was in receivership. It was taken over by the Midland Railway, and was shut in 1966 as part of the Beeching closures, but you can still spot remains of its stations and sidings along the trail. The far end of the trail runs parallel to the disused Stroudwater canal which once linked Stroud to the River Severn.

WOODCHESTER PARK & MANSION

Woodchester Mansion was designed by local architect, Benjamin Bucknell. It was begun, but never finished. The workmen walked out leaving sections of the house open to the sky, doors leading nowhere, and corridors ending in mid-air. For many years it stood decaying in its secluded valley. Now it is being restored although it will never be finished. For a house with so many gruesome gargoyles, it is perhaps not surprising to discover that it is home to one of the country's largest colonies of rare Greater Horseshoe bats, and some sinister ghost stories. The mansion is open for guided tours from 11 am to 4 pm on selected weekends from April to October (ring 01453 750457 or visit their website at www.the-mansion.co.uk). To get to the mansion you should either walk down the 1 mile long drive or take a free mini-bus from the Coaley Peak picnic site. An entrance fee is charged.

The 19th-century Park is a Site of Special Scientific Interest comprising five lakes and paths through the secret valley. It is run by the National Trust and is open daily from 9 am to 8 pm (May to September) and 9 am to 5 pm (October to March). An entrance fee is charged for non-members. The entrance to the park is on the route, on the road between Coaley Peak and Nympsfield.

THE COTSWOLD/SEVERN LONG BARROWS
Hetty Pegler's Tump and the Nympsfield long barrow are both examples of more than 100 such barrows located all over the Severn Valley and Cotswold area. They are generally from 5,000 to 5,500 years old.

Wotton-under-Edge and the Vale of Berkeley

22½ miles

The historic town of Wotton-under-Edge nestles under the Cotswold escarpment, and the route starts by making its way to North Nibley, on the escarpment edge, where you can walk up to and enjoy immense views from the Tyndale Monument. From here the route descends into the Vale of Berkeley and into Berkeley itself. Visit the Norman castle-cum-stately home or the Jenner Museum, a fascinating museum dedicated to the father of immunology. The route then meanders through the flat Severn flood plain before returning to Wotton-under-Edge along some delightfully quiet roads offering impressive views back to the escarpment.

Map: OS Landranger 162 Gloucester and Forest of Dean area (GR 755934).

Starting point: This ride starts out from the free long-stay car park at the Civic Centre which is located to the south of the B4060 (Gloucester Street) near the centre of Wotton-under-Edge.

Refreshments: Wotton is well supplied with teashops and pubs. In Berkeley, there is a teashop at the castle serving light lunches and refreshments. Light lunches are also available at the coffee and craft shop on High Street, and pub meals at the Berkeley Arms.

The route: The ride is moderately hilly especially at the beginning and end where there are climbs to the top of the escarpment at North Nibley and later from the Severn flood plain back to Wotton-under-Edge. The middle section of the ride is flat.

From the long-stay car park, stand facing the Civic Centre. Take the footpath to your right (signed Bradley Street/Town Centre) to Bradley Street. **Turn R** heading away from the town centre. **Bear R** and at the T-junction with the B4060 **turn L** (not signed). Soon **turn L** (signed Bradley Green). At the T-junction, **turn R** (signed Dursley/North Nibley). Continue on this road until it meets the B4060 at a T-junction and **turn L** (signed North Nibley/Dursley). Soon you will pass the village sign for North Nibley. Almost immediately (before the telephone box) there is a footpath off to the right to the Tyndale Monument. The walk is a steep one of about

The Norman ramparts, Berkeley Castle

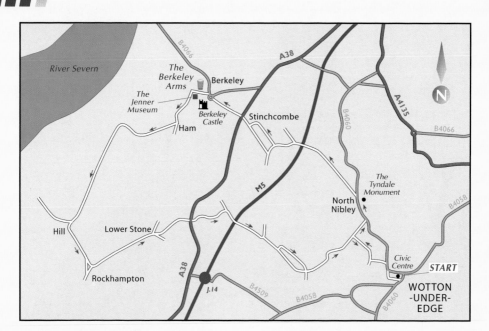

¼ mile, but on a fine day you can see Wales.

At the crossroads in North Nibley, **turn L** (The Street, not signed). **Bear R** by the church (signed Nibley Green/Blanchworth). Descend a steep hill and **bear L** then **bear R** (signed Berkeley). After crossing over the M5, **turn L** (signed Damery/Lower Wick). Cross the railway and immediately **turn R** (not signed, and despite the vegetation in it, yes it is a road!). At the T-junction, **turn R** (not signed) and at the T-junction with the A38 (take care!), **turn R** (signed Gloucester) and immediately **turn L** (signed Sharpness/Berkeley). **Turn L** at the T-junction (signed Berkeley/Sharpness) and go straight on at the roundabout (signed Berkeley). You will soon pass the

entrance to Berkeley Castle on your left and shortly afterwards enter Berkeley itself.

When you are ready to continue, **turn L** down High Street (signed The Jenner Museum). Ride into the village of Ham and **turn R** (signed Clapton/Bevington Hill, Cycle Route 41). Keep on this road following the blue signs for cycle route 41. Ride through Hill (which is flat!). **Turn L** (signed Rockhampton/Thornbury) and leave route 41. Ride into Rockhampton and **turn L** (not signed) and at the following crossroads **turn L** (signed Berkeley/Lower Stone). In Lower Stone, **turn R** (signed Stone/Falfield) and soon **bear L** (signed Stone). At the T-junction with the A38 (take care!) **turn R** (signed Bristol) and soon

Berkeley Castle

turn **L** (not signed, but unsuitable for heavy vehicles).

This lovely road is narrow and after crossing the Little Avon River it may be gravel-covered, so take care. At the T-junction, **turn R** (signed Damery) and cross the M5 again. Climb up through a wood and **turn R** (signed Huntingford/Charfield). You should soon be able to see the Tyndale Monument in the distance. **Turn L** (signed North Nibley/Durlsey) and pass under the railway. At the crossroads, **turn L** (signed Howley/North Nibley) and at the T-junction **turn R** (signed Kingswood/Charfield). **Turn L** (signed Wotton-under-Edge) and climb a steep hill. At the T-junction at the top, **turn R** (not signed) and

then **turn R** (signed unsuitable for heavy vehicles). This road bends left and turns into Bradley Street. The footpath to the Civic Centre car park is near the bottom of the road on the left.

● ●

WOTTON-UNDER-EDGE

Wotton-under-Edge is an unpretentious and friendly little town. A walk around its centre will reveal many pleasant old buildings, including three sets of almshouses and many small family-run shops. There is a small museum located along with the Tourist Information Centre in The Chipping. Sir Isaac Pitman taught at the nonconformist British School in the town. It was while he was living here that he invented his system of shorthand or phonography as he called it. Another famous son of the area is William Tyndale who was born in 1484 possibly in North Nibley. He held the then controversial view that the Bible should be published in English, something which would have removed the priesthood's monopoly on its interpretation, and was therefore regarded as little short of treasonable. Unable to achieve publication in this country he was forced to move to mainland Europe, where his translation was published in 1526. After unsuccessful attempts to lure him back to Britain, he was eventually murdered near Brussels. The Tyndale Monument, a 111 foot high cenotaph, was erected in 1863 and now dominates this section of escarpment.

BERKELEY CASTLE
The Norman castle at Berkeley has, in the 24 generations since its completion in 1153, been slowly transformed from a forbidding fortress into a family home. It and the Berkeley family who own it have played their part in the history of England, and the contents of the castle, with its historic Great Hall, state apartments, and dungeon where Edward II was murdered in 1327 can't fail to fascinate. The castle is surrounded by sweeping lawns and terraced Elizabethan gardens which may also be visited. The castle and gardens are open at selected times from April to October. For exact details please ring 01453 810332. An entrance fee is charged for castle, gardens and butterfly farm.

THE EDWARD JENNER MUSEUM
Edward Jenner was born in Berkeley in 1749 and after training as a surgeon in London returned to Berkeley, and 'The Chantry' where he was to spend the rest of his life. The museum charts the life and career of Jenner himself, and also the path to the eradication of smallpox and the subsequent development of immunology. In the museum, Jenner comes across as an extraordinary man who not only invented immunology, but also contributed to our understanding of the nesting habits of cuckoos, the hibernation of hedgehogs and was a keen geologist and fossil hunter. Incidentally he was also probably the first person in Britain to fly in a hot-air balloon. Quite a career for a country doctor!

19

Tetbury: A Right Royal Ride!

22 miles

The market town of Tetbury lies in an area currently dominated by royal estates. The route starts climbing gently up to Minchinhampton Common, a large expanse of common land offering stunning views of the Stroud, Golden and Nailsworth valleys, a perfect place for flying kites and having picnics. The return journey takes you through Minchinhampton itself and on to Avening before a short climb leaves you descending gently back towards Tetbury, passing Chavenage House, a wonderful Elizabethan/Jacobean mansion.

Maps: OS Landranger 163 Cheltenham and Cirencester and 162 Gloucester and Forest of Dean area. Alternatively the entire route is to be found on OS Touring Map 8 The Cotswolds (GR 890931).

Starting point: The ride starts from the Market Hall, the unmistakable market cross in the heart of Tetbury. Long-stay parking is located slightly to the north-east of the town centre off the Cirencester road.

Refreshments: Tetbury has several pubs and a number of teashops located near its centre. In nice weather what could be better than a picnic amid the flowers on Minchinhampton Common?

The route: Although this route takes the rider up onto the heights of Minchinhampton Common, the climb from Tetbury is a relatively gentle one. The roads through the common can be busy on summer weekends, and so extra care must be taken.

From the Market Hall, stand facing the Snooty Fox Hotel. **Turn R** along the B4014 (signed Malmesbury). Follow this road into the village of Long Newnton and there **turn L** (signed Church/Crudwell/Cirencester). At the T-junction with the A433 **turn R** (signed Cirencester) and soon **turn L** (not signed). At the next T-junction, **turn R** (signed Avening/Cherington) and soon

bear **R** (signed Cherington). In Cherington, **turn L** (signed Avening). Soon **turn R** down a steep wooded hill (look out for gravel!) with a lake to your left (signed Hampton Fields/Stroud). **Turn R** at crossroads in Hampton Fields (signed Chalford/Stroud). Ride straight through Crackstone and at the T-junction, **turn L** (signed Minchinhampton/Stroud). Soon you will cross a cattle grid

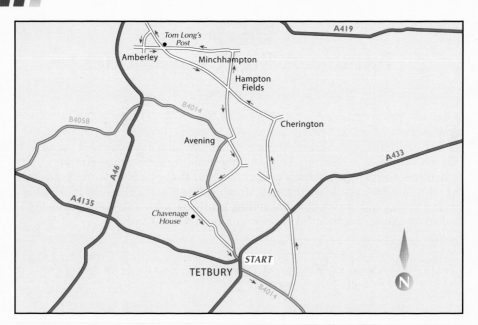

and enter the common.

Keep straight on at Tom Long's Post where six roads join. Half a mile further on **turn L** (signed Amberley). Ride through Amberley and **turn L** at the T-junction (signed Minchinhampton). You will soon find yourself approaching Tom Long's Post from another direction. At the T-junction, **turn L** (signed Cirencester/Stroud) and immediately **turn R** (signed Minchinhampton Town Centre). Ride straight through Minchinhampton and Hampton Fields and on into Avening. **Turn L** next to the Cross Inn (Star Lane, not signed) and climb the hill. **Turn R** on a left-hand bend (signed Chavenage).

Go straight on at the crossroads (signed Chavenage House) and at the T-junction, **turn L** (signed Chavenage House). The entrance to the house is soon passed on your right. Coast down into Tetbury. At the T-junction **turn R** (not signed) and soon **turn R** into Long Street and return to the Market Hall.

● ●

TETBURY

Tetbury is a quiet Cotswold town, steeped in history, and owing to its lack of a natural water supply, relatively untouched by the Industrial Revolution. The first written records of the town describe it as a Saxon monastery under the control of the Abbess Tetta. It soon developed into a centre of Cotswold wool and held one of the best wool and yarn markets in the country. Today it is well worth exploring on foot as it has many historical buildings including the Market House (1655), one of the finest examples of a pillared Cotswold market house (and still used for Wednesday

The Market Hall, Tetbury

markets), the Chipping Steps, where farm labourers and domestic staff offered themselves for hiring, Gumstool Hill, ancient street and site of the annual woolsack races, and the unusual Georgian gothic church of St Mary. Today it is also well-known for its Royal Estates. Both Prince Charles and the Princess Royal have estates within 5 miles of the town.

CHAVENAGE HOUSE

Chavenage House is an unspoiled Elizabethan and Jacobean mansion set in the rolling countryside north of Tetbury. It retains many of its original features including much Elizabethan decorative wooden panelling, possibly because it has not been 'improved' as a result of constantly changing ownership. Only two families have owned it since it was

completed by Edward Stephens in 1576. During the Civil War, the house was owned by Colonel Nathaniel Stephens, a member of the Privy Council. Legend has it that he was placed under a curse by his daughter after having been persuaded by Cromwell's son-in-law Henry Ireton to support the King's execution. Shortly afterwards he was taken terminally ill, and on his death, it is said that a hearse drew up at the manor driven by a headless man who on driving away with the colonel's body (which had risen from its coffin) assumed the shape of the executed King. Tours of the house, often taken by members of the Lowsley-Williams family (the present owners), are held on Thursdays and Sundays between May and September from 2 pm to 5 pm and are fascinating and highly recommended.

20

Saxon Malmesbury and the Avon Valley

26 miles

This gentle ride starts and finishes in the town of Malmesbury in Wiltshire, the site of a magnificent Norman abbey. The ride explores the Avon valley to the south-west and circumnavigates the Duke of Beaufort's estate at Badminton before returning through the pleasant villages of Sherston and Shipton Moyne. The magnificent Westonbirt Arboretum may be visited during a short detour. This is a lovely scenic route, especially in the summer when the many wide verges are awash with yellow buttercups, pink campion, white stitchwort and blue cranesbill.

> **Maps:** OS Landranger 173 Swindon, Devizes and surrounding area. The route just impinges on OS Landranger 172 Bristol and Bath but it is not really necessary to have this map (GR 933873).
>
> **Starting point:** The ride starts from the Market Cross in the centre of Malmesbury, located just west of the A429 (Cirencester to Chippenham) road, 12 miles south-west of Cirencester. The free long-stay car park is located off the B4014 (Tetbury Road) just to the north of the town centre and is well signed.
>
> **Refreshments:** There are many places to eat in Malmesbury. Along the route there are not many possibilities until Sherston where the Rattlebone and Carpenter's Arms pubs serve food, and during the week the coffee shop in the post-office serves sandwiches and other light snacks. If you detour to Westonbirt, the Arboretum has a restaurant, or alternatively you can picnic in arboreal splendour.
>
> **The route:** Although the ride is the longest in the book, it is paradoxically one of the easiest because it is flat.

To get to the starting point from the car park, walk over the bridge at the far end of the car park and follow the wheelchair access signs which bring you out on the B-road. **Turn L** and cycle past the Abbey, **bear L** by the tower and the Market Cross is immediately to your left.

From the Market Cross, **turn R** (signed Gloucester). At The Triangle, **turn L** (signed Sherston, B4040). **Turn L** (signed Foxley/ Norton). In Foxley, turn L (signed Norton/Hullavington, Wiltshire Cycleway). **Bear R** (signed Norton/Hullavington) and ride into Norton and **bear L** crossing a usually dry ford (signed

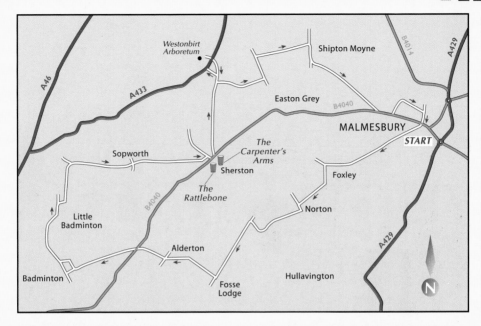

Hullavington/Sherston). **Turn R** at the T-junction (signed Sherston). On a right-hand bend, **turn L** (signed Farleaze). At the next T-junction **turn R** (not signed, but the other way is a No Through Road). At the following T-junction, **turn L** (not signed, but you have now joined the Romans on the Fosse Way).

Turn R (signed Alderton/ Luckington) opposite the bizarre-looking Fosse Lodge. **Turn L** (signed Alderton) and ride into the village passing the village pond stocked with some surprisingly exotic inhabitants. Keep straight ahead (signed Badminton). At the T-junction **turn L** (signed Acton Turville/Badminton) and soon **turn R** (signed Badminton). Along this stretch of road you will get your

only good views of the house. On entering Badminton village, **turn R** (not signed, Hayes Lane). At the T-junction **turn L** (not signed) and at the next T-junction **turn R** (sign unclear but for Little Badminton). Ride under a bridge and on and through Little Badminton. **Turn R** through two stone gateposts with rusting iron gates (not signed, don't worry this is an official road). Soon the road bends to the left leaving you riding along a straight road lined with sycamore trees.

At the T-junction, **turn R** into a wood (not signed). Go straight ahead at the crossroads and descend and climb gently into Sherston. **Turn R** at the crossroads (signed Malmesbury). **Turn L** opposite the Rattlebone pub. The centre of Sherston is off to the

Malmesbury Abbey

right and is well worth exploring. On leaving the village **turn L** at the crossroads (signed Westonbirt/ Tetbury). After about 1½ miles there is an unsigned right-hand turn. If you want to return straight to Malmesbury, **turn R** (not signed).

If you wish to visit Westonbirt Arboretum (1½ mile detour) keep straight ahead and then **bear L** (signed Didmarton/Tetbury/ Arboretum). At the T-junction with the A433, carefully **turn R** (signed Cirencester) and soon **turn L** at the entrance to the Arboretum. On leaving return to the A433 and **turn R** (signed Bath) and immediately **turn L** (signed Westonbirt Village). Keep straight

ahead and **turn L** (not signed) to rejoin the main route.

Turn L at the T-junction and then **turn R** opposite an estate lodge (the first of two right-hand turns close together). Soon **turn R** at a T-junction (not signed). **Turn R** at another T-junction and ride into Shipton Moyne. **Bear L** (signed Malmesbury). At the T-junction with the B4040, **turn L** (signed Malmesbury) and **turn L** at the top of a short rise (signed Brokenborough). **Turn R** (signed Malmesbury) and ride alongside the River Ingleburn. At the T-junction in Malmesbury, **turn L** and then **turn L** again to return to the long-stay car park. Alternatively **turn R** to return to the Market

Cross (signed Town Centre). **Turn L** at The Triangle into the 20 mph zone. Pass the Abbey on your left, **bear L** by the tower to return to the Market Cross.

● ●

MALMESBURY

Malmesbury is a town steeped in history, perched on high ground between the rivers Avon and Ingleburn. It claims to be the oldest borough in the country, having been granted its charter in AD 880, by King Alfred. The Abbey still dominates the town, even though it is currently only one third the size of the original Norman Benedictine abbey. It is believed to have been founded in the 7th century, and the Norman abbey dates from 1180. The two rivers provided the motive power for a thriving woollen industry which, when it declined in the 17th century, was replaced by a lace and silk industry the profits from which paid for many of the present buildings. If you would like to find out more, why not visit the Athelstan Museum located in the Town Hall in Cross Hayes, a square just to the south of the Market Cross. It is open Tuesdays to Saturdays 10 am to 2 pm.

WESTONBIRT ARBORETUM

Westonbirt Arboretum contains a collection of some 18,000 trees from all over the world which have been planted in 600 acres of rolling Cotswold countryside from 1829 to the present. It is a lovely place to visit at any time of the year. However, spectacular displays of rhododendrons, azaleas and wild flowers can be seen from March till June. The Arboretum is also justifiably famous for its spectacular display of autumn colours from September to early November, including its famous acer glade.

A family outing on the River Ingleburn

FURTHER INFORMATION

The Cyclists' Touring Club is the national organisation which represents and campaigns for the interests of all cyclists, whether they ride to work or ride around the world. The club has touring and technical departments to help with all your cycling queries, and issues a bimonthly magazine to all its members. In the area covered by this book there are also local CTC groups which organise a variety of led day and half-day rides. All these groups welcome new riders. Rides are led by experienced local cyclists on quiet country roads. If you have enjoyed the rides in this book, why not make contact with your local group and enjoy riding with like-minded people? If you would like to find out more about the CTC, and your local groups contact the national headquarters by phone or email (see below)

Finally we would both like to thank all our friends in the Oxfordshire CTC and in particular Stephen Lee who helped ride many of the routes and never complained when he was used as a photographic model.

CTC (CYCLISTS' TOURING CLUB) NATIONAL HEADQUARTERS
Telephone (Help Desk): 01483 417217
Email: Cycling@ctc.org.uk
Website: www.ctc.org.uk